Learner-Centered Design

Learner-Centered Design

A Cognitive

View of

Managing

Complexity in

Product,

Information, and

Environmental

Design

Wayne Reeves

Sage Publications, Inc.
International Educational and Professional Publisher
Thousand Oaks ■ London ■ New Delhi

For information:

Sage Publications, Inc.
2455 Teller Road
Thousand Oaks, California 91320
E-mail: order@sagepub.com

Sage Publications Ltd.
6 Bonhill Street
London EC2A 4PU
United Kingdom

Sage Publications India Pvt. Ltd.
M-32 Market
Greater Kailash I
New Delhi 110 048 India

Printed in the United States of America

Library of Congress Cataloging-in-Publication Data

Reeves, Wayne, W.
     Learner-centered design: A cognitive view of managing complexity
in product, information, and environmental design / by Wayne Reeves.
       p.   cm.
    Includes bibliographical references (p.   ) and index.
    ISBN 0-7619-0726-2 (cloth) — ISBN 0-7619-0727-0 (pbk.)
    1. Learning, Psychology of.   2. Human information processing.
    3. Complexity (Philosophy).   4. Cognitive science.   5. Categorization
(Psychology).   I. Title.
    BF318.R44   1999
    153.1é5—dc21   99-26072

This book is printed on acid-free paper.

99 00 01 02 03 04 05 7 6 5 4 3 2 1

Acquisition Editor:	Peter Labella
Editorial Assistant:	Renée Piernot
Production Editor:	Denise Santoyo
Editorial Assistant:	Nevair Kabakian
Cover Designer:	Candice Harman

Dedication

To Doug Engelbart, for encouraging an unrelenting exploration of the future and our ability to augment the human capacity for understanding in the face of overwhelming complexity.

Contents

Preface: Consumers and Complexity

> In the long run we can master change not through force or fear, but only through the free work of an understanding mind.
>
> —Robert F. Kennedy

Recent polls have shown that about 75% of the people in the United States feel that life is too complicated and that technology contributes to that complexity in a significant manner. In keeping with this sense of being overwhelmed, we have also recently seen the trend in the definition of success move from the "ability to travel" to simply "being in control of one's life." Both of these growing trends are being addressed by advertisers pitching the simplicity or simplifying nature of their products. This has been the response of advertisers. What will be the response of the design world? This book is about an approach to design that can substantially lessen the cognitive complexity of a wide range of consumer products from ecommerce to workspaces. It is, of course, this actual new design of products, and not advertising slogans, that will ultimately ensure future competitiveness and true customer satisfaction.

COMPLEXITY AND OUR AGE

What is the correct moniker for this age? Some people have called it the Space Age or the Electronics Age or the postmodern era. Bell (1973) has often referred to it as the Postindustrial Information Age, and our society has been referred to as a postindustrial society. Just as Gergen (1991) bemoaned the use of the word *postmodern* because the term fails to specify any essence (defining itself merely as post) I believe that there is an essence to our era: complexity. We are living in the Age of Complexity. The fundamental task of this era is to address the scientific, technological, political, economic, psychological, and sociological complexity that threatens to overwhelm us. This book addresses a fundamental part of that overall task, the role of design, for it is inadequate design that contributes so much complexity to our daily lives.

This study of complexity and the design of products, information, and environments focuses on managing cognitive complexity: those elements and forces in our environment and society that add both a necessary and an unnecessary neural load to most of the aspects of our postindustrial lives. The basic weapon in our arsenal will be the practical aspects of what we have learned from 30 years of cognitive research about learning and understanding. To that powerful, insightful weapon I will add a fuller conceptualization of the nature of complexity and the design evaluation techniques pioneered by Nielsen (1995), Cooper (1999), and others.

This book is concerned with how to manage complexity and how we can use the design of products, information, and workspaces to aid in this management. In a sense, we are in a race with complexity. Will it overwhelm our capacity to deal with it, as is increasingly the case today, or will we use what we are learning in the cognitive and information sciences to stave off the chaos? Actually, chaos theory, or the science of the complex itself, may give us some insight into the future of learning and thinking and how scaffolding, or supporting understanding as a primary goal of design, could be the most effective strategy for the management of complexity in the long run. From these insights, and associated ones from distributed cognition, perhaps we will see a significant change in our paradigm of learning, instruction, and what constitutes understanding. Perhaps it will support the growing application of cognitive science research in education (Bruer, 1993). I say this because chaos theory, like the trajectory of cognitive science research, supports the concept of a complex world not reducible to artificial simplicities and because successful theories about our world often end up influencing our educational philosophies.

When learning theory was developed under the Newtonian paradigm of the world, learning was considered mechanical, behavioral, and individual. Learning systems were geared to stimulus-response activity, rote rehearsal, and simple association. To an extent, the paradigm shift to quantum mechanics and relativity lagged in its effect on learning theory. The quantum world was seen as more complex, more probabilistic and less directly observable, and this gained only partial translation into educational styles. But we have eventually moved to a point where learning is considered in terms of the internal functions of an active, constructive, motivated mind. At the same time, the idea of what constitutes learning has grown broader and more flexible than the all-too-brittle mechanistic perspective. We are currently engaged in an eclectic synthesis of learning by scaffolding, collaboration, narrative, discovery, critical engagement, and heuristic example, as well as the more algorithmic, observational, and didactic informing methods. And all of these efforts have an impact on the methods of modern design. It is debatable whether people set out to consciously create learning theories that reflect the received scientific view of the time, but we are already experiencing a new shift in learning based on chaos theory's simpler, even more demonstrative view of the underlying order of our world. If we choose to take conscious strides to evolve our learning theory, informed by our understanding of how the world operates, we may have a chance of getting ahead of the evolutionary learning curve in our design processes as well because design practice flows from our educational models.

Long before mathematicians discovered that the world sits on the edge of chaos, the average person already saw that life could be overwhelmingly complex. We could see that many of the more difficult problems would remain untouched and left to future generations that would be just as inadequately prepared to solve them. We see the exacerbated effect of this evolution of complexity in our postindustrial information societies, but the effects are not isolated there. Technology has linked problems on a global basis, making them increasingly harder to visualize, let alone resolve.

We need an ongoing collaborative research effort for the development of newly informed learning systems and fully distributed information, product, and workspace design principles that will be capable of coping with the new set of problem-solving and decision-making complexities that, as the science of complexity itself contends, will arise irresistibly and irreversibly in the future (Cohen & Stewart, 1994; Goerner, 1990; Nicolis & Prigogine, 1989).

We cannot afford to ignore the rising cognitive complexity within our society and to pass it on unmanaged to future generations. This would be a growing deficit in our world's problem-solving capacity that we cannot afford to bequeath to our children. Three points seem clear:

1. Complexity will follow an evolutionary projection (Laszlo, 1987; Prigogine & Stengers, 1984).

2. The key to future information, product, and workspace design is a focus on the management of complexity at the cognitive level (individual and distributed) (Cohen & Stewart, 1994; Reeves, 1996).

3. Understanding and design must be taken as a systemic distributed event comprising the quality of the transfer of information between object or workspace and user; the consumer's or learner's information-seeking and knowledge-building capacity; and and the presence of learner-centered interfaces and other knowledge management tools aimed at scaffolding the construction of useful mental models (Banathy, 1991; Collins & Mangieri, 1992; Kuhlthau, 1991; Marchionini, 1995; Norman,

1988; Norman and Spohrer, 1996; Soloway, Guzdial, & Hay 1994; Soloway & Pryor, 1996).

In developing a general-purpose learner-centered design (LCD) scheme, this book is organized around the following activities:

1. Building a model of the origins and characteristics of cognitive complexity, including complexity-simplicity word-pair scales

2. Proposing an LCD evaluation *tool kit*

3. Reviewing matched pairs of cognitive and information science topics in a cognitive hierarchy

4. Extracting and presenting from this review the content of the LCD evaluation tools and design principles

My particular approach is transdisciplinary in an attempt to bridge the already interdisciplinary fields of information science and cognitive science. Cognitive science supplies much of the philosophical and psychological foundations for the LCD scheme, and information science supplies many of the implications of application and implementation. And, as our discussions will exemplify, there are basic insights from each science that should be fruitful for the other, for both are ultimately engaged in an endeavor to better understand and manage human information and knowledge processing.

Thus, my task in *Learner-Centered Design* is to create an awareness of "managing complexity" as a fundamental design issue, to use cognitive insights to view all consumers as learners, and to expose the unique opportunity that design has in creating and sustaining human performance and organizational competitiveness.

Wayne W. Reeves
Sunnyvale, CA

Acknowledgments

Many people have contributed to making this book possible and guiding me in the management of its complexity. I would like to thank Professors Blanche Woolls, Stuart Sutton, Bill Fisher, David Loertscher, and Ruth Hafter of the School of Library and Information Science (SLIS) at San Jose State University (SJSU) for their ongoing encouragement and an opportunity to give the first course based on this material; Professor Christine Borgman of the University of California, Los Angeles, for the right word at the right time; Dr. Albert Lowe and David Wick of Sun Microsystems for their recognition of the value of learner-centered design in the corporate world; Drs. Doug Engelbart from the Bootstrap Institute; Donald Norman, Richard Wurman, Jakob Nielsen, and Robert Sternberg for their prodigious work in design, cognition, and learning that continues to inspire the development of my own creative processes; Sarah Rice for her outstanding research assistance from beginning to end; Anise Kirkpatrick for her special research efforts; and Paul Perrotta of Sequoia Document Design for his immeasurable editorial and graphic assistance. I would especially like to thank my editor at Sage, Peter Labella, my reviewers for their very helpful suggestions, and the students at SJSU SLIS, for their courage and encouragement in participating in the various stages of this eclectic and complex proposal for the future of product, workspace, and information design.

1

Introduction

How is society doing in adapting technology to the minds of its users? Badly.... The signs are clear from confusion and difficulty in using household and office appliances....When technology is not designed from a human-centered point of view, it doesn't reduce the incidence ... nor minimize the impact when errors occur.

—Donald Norman

Learner-Centered Design (LCD) is based on a newly emerging view of human beings and the purpose of design—a view strongly affected by the cognitive (individual and distributed) revolution of the last 30 years. Even though we may have considered it only natural to think of ourselves as thinking beings, we have only recently begun to understand the nature and active potential of our thinking capacity. It is even more recent that we have actually begun to trust that capacity and sought to implement its implications in real-world settings. LCD is based on those elements of design that help to achieve understanding. It is thus based on the nexus of research and real-world experience exemplified by the work of Norman (1986, 1993) and Wurman (1989, 1997), research into distributed cognition (Pea, 1993), and the constructivist theory of instruction (Bruer, 1993; Marshall, 1995; Piaget, 1954; Soloway et al., 1994). What is positive for LCD is that excellent examples of it already exist in growing abundance in school curricula, computer learning systems, consumer products, and information design. In this book, we will have an opportunity to point to many of these as we describe the LCD principles involved (see Wurman, 1997, *Information Architects*).

Given this approach to LCD, for whom is this book intended? This book is not for use just by those designing educationally oriented computer learning systems. Even though there is a growing faction of support for LCD in the computer industry, LCD is a general approach to design that encompasses a broad spectrum of design efforts wherever distributed human-object inter-action is involved. This book is aimed at all designers: designers of products, designers of work environments, and designers of information ("information architects") and information systems. It is aimed at such a broad audience for three reasons: (a) It is focused on the cognitive impact of design for customers, consumers, students, workers, and others of all ages and all motivations; (b) it considers these users, students, and consumers as active engaged learners, as beings whose main motivation is to understand the products and information presented in and flowing through their environments; and (c) it considers the use and functional value of all product design to be based on the effective communication of information from the product or through the workspace to those using the product or working in that space. It considers scaffolding, or support of understanding, to be essential in all design, not just the design of systems actively engaged in training on a particular task, skill, or subject. Successful design now and in the future will be based on the successful communication of product information in terms of (a) the ease of getting started with the product's intended purpose, (b) the ease of sustained use, and (c) the ease of content understanding (content such as that found in a web site, a map, a digital library, a museum kiosk, a computer, or a home appliance).

Much design has rightly concerned itself with learnability (or the initial difficulty in learning how to use an application, space, or product) and usability (the ease of use of a system or product over time). LCD extends these concerns to include understandability. Understandability includes an extension of what it means for a system to be usable, an extension that includes the thoughtful design of content (facts, examples, help aids, and so on) being displayed or communicated by the designed artifact. Take, for example, a television set of the 1960s or 1970s. Commonly, this design did not need "understandability" included in its design because one gained adequate understanding from good usability principles. But what happens when we move that television to the digital age of complex multifunctionality, of Internet connections, DVDs, VCRs, and camcorder attachments? Now more information needs to be communicated through the design. Some of the responsibility for that increased communication can be taken up by extensions of usability elements, but some of it will need to be borne by the design of the information content presented. LCD, with its emphasis on understandability, takes responsibility for both that extension of usability and the design of the content. For learnability, usability, and understandability to be optimally applied in LCD, the full range of cognitive principles (not just the rules of perception or model building) must be employed to ensure that users under-stand how to use the product or space and that they also understand any actual "content" provided in or displayed by that product or workspace (environment). For conciseness, I will call the object of design for this book, that combines users with products, information, or environmentals, *inter-active-information-fields*. An interactive-information-field, or more concisely an information-field, as a target of design is, in a distributed cognitive sense, a focus on the total product-user interaction. LCD takes as its unique responsibility and goal a more equal distribution of the neural load for using and understanding any justifiably complex product or space. Tool- or technology-centered design placed the total burden of usability on the individual users and their cognitive capacities. User-centered design began to make the shift of the neural load to the designed product. Better design, more cognitively aware design, helped users to intuitively figure out what to do.

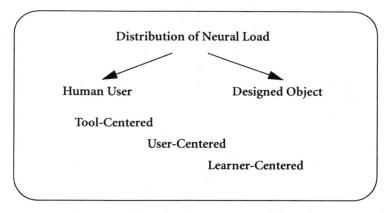

Figure 1.1.   The shift of understandability and the neural load from the user to the designed artifact.

Finally, in LCD we complete the shift—the distribution—of the neural load of usability and understanding away from the user and toward the designed product. Thus, LCD is concerned with the design of rebalanced information-fields, broadly defined, encompassing the important use of the LCD concept in computer-human-interaction research (Soloway et al., 1994). That being said, most of the discussions in this book are centered on information-intense product designs because they provide excellent examples of the principles we are trying to explore for the broader world of design. This book is essentially part reference and part pointer, including thought-provoking research and pointing to further experimentation and inquiry. It is a forward-looking work with a practical proposal: a set of enhanced information-field (product, environmental, and information) design guidelines and evaluative tools that address cognitive complexity (factors that affect our ability to understand). The time is right for such a heightened sensibility in design because of what we have learned over the last 30 years of cognitive research and the pressing need

to get ahead of the hyperabundance curve and the accumulation of information and knowledge in our environment.

What is the common characteristic of all interactive-information-fields?
Information-fields represent a potential for communication in the interaction
between the appliance and its user. An information-field is an extended
cognitive frame of reference that systemically ties the product, tool, or
workspace to the user of that product, or tool, or space. Because most of the
appliances we use every day require learning and understanding to be used
effectively, information-fields apply to these product interactions as well as to
more obvious learning situations. In a sense then, an information-field is
similar to Zuboff's concept of an *informate*, described by Norman (1993) as a
reflective cognitive artifact: "An informating system is a reflective cognitive
artifact that gives people access to the knowledge they need to make informed,
intelligent decisions" (pp. 226–227). This includes everything from the design
of virtual college courses on the Web, explanatory kiosks systems in cities and
in museums, and traditional classroom curricula to educational software,
digital libraries, intranet knowledge management systems, commercial
products (cellular phones, car navigation systems, vcrs), and corporate
workspaces. The question that motivates this book is, "Why aren't all
commercial products, information, and workspaces designed as 'informating'
systems—as learner-centered systems taking advantage of distributing the
cognitive load of understanding between the object and the individual?" Why
are products not designed with the facilitation of user understanding in mind?
For example, why are we still dealing with a vcr's flashing timer, meaningless
error messages, call direction systems that lead nowhere, a huge secondary
market in books explaining major computer applications, incompatibility
between computer types, and the myriad other product elements and structures that plague our everyday cognitive lives (see Norman, 1988)? This work
is dedicated to information-field design that facilitates individual understanding and takes the extra responsibility of being "instructionally minded."

Further, I take complexity as the central factor in barriers to learning and
understanding. Thus, I focus on design issues that affect the management of
cognitive complexity in the triune aspects of the modern learning process: (a)
learning how to use an information-field, (b) understanding how it operates,
and (c) learning and understanding the content or knowledge that an information-field intends to provide. It is mostly in the last sense that the approach
of this book to lcd differs from purely user-centered system design. This book
is meant to provide an increasingly necessary foundation for discussion of this
design view because the enhanced requirements of lcd will surely add another
level of difficulty to the design and evaluation of all systems. But it is important
that the burden of extra effort reside with the designer and not with the public
that uses the designed products. Where does this book fit within the tradition
of all those other excellent product, interface, and information design books?

Over a decade ago, interface design was forever changed with the introduction of Norman and Draper's *User Centered System Design* (1986). This was followed a few years later by Norman's broadly influential look at design in general, *The Psychology of Everyday Things* (1988), and his *Things That Make Us Smart* (1993). Along with these came two other pivotal information design books, Tufte's *Envisioning Information* (1990) and Mullet and Sano's *Designing Visual Interfaces* (1995). The influence of these books was due in no small part to their application of principles of cognitive science to the practice of design. I take the same approach in this work. I want to take principles of cognitive science and information science and create guidelines for designers who face specific information-field design issues.

To help get a handle on the outlook of this book, let me compare it to Norman's approach in *The Psychology of Everyday Things*. First, in that book, Norman extended the standard of computer interface design to the design of a wide variety of everyday objects: workspaces, menus, doorways, and so on. As stated above, my scope is equally broad, but I will, for the most part, use examples from the design of complex information-rich entities. Second, whereas Norman focused on poor or inadequate design as a major source of complexity for the user, I want to take a slightly different vector and expand the discussion of the sources of complexity to include all the major sources of cognitive complexity faced by learners (see Chapter 2). Third, my approach to the presentation of the material is also quite different. Norman's approach is clearly and effectively based on examples from real life. My mode of presentation consists of linking areas of parallel research in cognitive science and information science, with examples of research being directed at some means of managing complexity. The research examples are presented in a sequence, chapter by chapter, that corresponds to moving up the human cognitive hierarchy from perception to reading comprehension. At each level, I point out lessons learned that are useful to LCD. The purpose of this process is to develop a set of LCD design principles that may be used for design or evaluation. I intend this work to be more a stimulant for discussion—supplying research directions, critical analysis, and practical application—than an attempt to prove a point or reach a certainty. Thus, the selection of material from the interdisciplinary cognitive and information sciences must be partial (with some areas completely overlooked). Why interleave cognitive science and information science research? To the broad venture described above, cognitive science contributes to our understanding of internal information processing, and information science contributes its understanding of external information processing. The common goals for these disciplines meet at the interface between the learner (consumer, worker, or student) and the information he or she is seeking. It is at the design of this interface that this work is focused. To meet the challenges presented by content-heavy information-fields, such as the Internet, corporate images, modern libraries, and museums, we must encourage information-fields to evolve from a technology-centered, or even user-centered, orientation to a more constructive LCD through the ever-growing influence of powerful and pertinent aspects of cognition that commingle with modern technology. It is the task of cognitive scientists, computer scientists, usability engineers, information architects, environmental designers, teachers, trainers, and students not only to converge on the problem of managing cognitive complexity but also to develop a framework for a new *literacy of complexity*. This work explores some of the issues surrounding that convergence in the form of learner-centered information-field design.

This book is also a response to Toffler's *Future Shock* (1970), Wurman's *Information Anxiety* (1989), and Gergen's *The Saturated Self* (1991), among others, each of which explains to us the increasingly overwhelming nature of the information explosion. In *Cognition and Complexity* (Reeves, 1996), I explored empowering individuals with cognitive strategies for managing the complexity of the modern learning process. In this work, the emphasis is on the design of a simpler, or at least more understandable and comprehensible, world that will have the power to reduce some of the cognitive complexity encountered by its inhabitants.

In summary, the focus of this book is fourfold:

1. Making it easier for people to interact as full partners with, and learn from, the information-fields that are designed to aid or inform them

2. Engaging designers with a proposal for managing a wide variety of sources of cognitive complexity

3. Comparing matched sets of cognitive and information science research, looking specifically for key material that applies to the management of complexity and facilitating understanding in information-field design

4. Proposing a set of heuristic guidelines for the design and evaluation of interactive-information-fields in the modern context

It is my intention to set an adjunct direction in the design of information-fields, namely an LCD direction that is flexible enough to incorporate new findings from the fields of human science while providing a framework for thinking about future design. I propose to move from user-centered design to an all-encompassing learner-centered design: in other words, to add to current design best practices a supplemental set of design principles that specifically target the management of cognitive complexity and understandability. Information-fields inherently bring with them a flood of information about the product, system, or workspace and its content. Only through the consideration of the user as a learner can information-fields be designed with elements that can handle this flood of system know-how and content know-what. LCD thus extends existing design by (a) facing comprehensive cognitive complexity as a central concern, (b) extending design to the system's information content, and (c) visualizing all users (students, workers, and consumers young and old) as distributed learners seeking understanding.

Previously (Reeves, 1996), I explored the cognitive basis for augmented learning under conditions of information hyperabundance. I used a generative heuristic approach to create a learning-to-learn heuristic that had the capacity to filter and bound irrelevant information while simultaneously transforming subject essentials into the building blocks of knowledge in understanding-oriented mental models. The goal was to provide the learner with the answers to three questions: "What do I know?" "What do I need to know?" and "How do I know if I know enough?" In fulfilling my purpose for this proposal, I follow a similar method of looking into the cognitive basis of many key elements of information-field design to discover a generative heuristic that could help guide the design process.

The method for uncovering these design elements (covered in Chapters 4 through 9) is described in the following general steps:

1. Consider an area of investigation in cognitive science that could be applied to the management of complexity, and explore its current state with information-field usability, learnability, and understandability in mind.

2. Find a complementary area of research in information science and describe its application to design.

3. Extract design principles.

4. Demonstrate how the principles manage complexity and how they affect the complexity scales described in Chapter 3.

5. Explain how the principles can be implemented in our LCD heuristic: that is, explain how the design element targets both system-use competency and system-content competency.

In this chapter I have introduced my conceptualizations of

1. LCD as a general design approach that emphasizes the complete cognitive nature of all humans (as workers, consumers, and lifelong learners) and their need to understand or comprehend the use of products and information in their environment. LCD in this general sense includes, but is not limited to, the design of learning systems particularly created to aid the learning process for students.

2. *Interactive-Information-fields* as a singular label combining the user in a distributed or shared systemic sense with three major objects of design—products, information systems of any type, and workspaces—

focusing on the interaction of learner and artifact as a single cognitive unit.

3.   *Understandability* as a LCD goal added to "initial learnability" and "long-term usability," focused on the ability of the product or workspace to implicitly communicate with and instruct (scaffold) the user as he or she interacts with it. Understandability is also the basic principle guiding the explicit design of product content (facts, examples, definitions, exercises) necessary to provide user understanding. It is also worthwhile to remember in doing LCD that current design practices are hardly responsive to the average learner; one can barely imagine the gulf between design and the needs of those with learning and other disabilities.

It is wonderful to note that understandability is already a growing goal of at least those information designers of the type listed in Wurman's (1997) *Information Architects*, and I am sure there are many other projects in other fields that are adopting this principle. The goal of this book is to place these current and future design efforts (including the cognitive aspects of participatory and contextual design strategies not explicitly discussed here) on an overt cognitive basis. A cognitive basis clearly displaying the aspects of complexity that they are managing (see "Soft Technologies" section in Norman, 1993). We will take the first step in this journey in the next chapter by introducing a more detailed analysis of cognitive complexity in the context of our general understanding of complexity per se. The purpose of that discussion is to distinguish between a variety of uses of the term while bringing a more critical and detailed awareness of cognitive complexity to the design process.

HOW THIS BOOK IS ORGANIZED

This book is divided into two parts:

- Part I discusses the nature of cognitive complexity, presents a complexity-related evaluative tool to be used in testing designs, and provides the conceptual framework for Part II.

- Part II describes how certain areas of cognitive and information science research can be applied to the management of complexity and the development of a set of LCD design principles.

Table 1.1 illustrates the organization of each of the two parts of the book.

Table 1.1. The Organization of This Book

Division	Chapter	Topic
Part I	Chapter 2. The Nature and Origins of Cognitive Complexity	Definition of complexity and description of the sources of cognitive complexity
	Chapter 3. Evaluating Cognitive Complexity	Use of cognitive complexity word-pairs as design scales
Part II	Chapter 4. Learner as Perceiver	Gestalt perception principles and information design
	Chapter 5. Learner as Model Builder	Representation, problem solving, and abstracting
	Chapter 6. Learner as Categorizer	Categorization and classification schemes
	Chapter 7. Learner as Searcher	Visualization and DQI
	Chapter 8. Learner as Expert	Expert problem solving, heuristics, and knowledge engineering
	Chapter 9. Learner as Student	Schema-based instruction and computer-based LCD
	Chapter 10. Tools for Learner-Centered Design	LCD *tool kit* and conclusion

PART I.
The Nature of Complexity

❧

2

The Nature and Origins of Cognitive Complexity

Some people maintain that increased complexity is an inevitable consequence of the times, and the role of computers is to manage complexity. Nonsense. Consciously throwing complexity at people (or computers) is an admission of ignorance, laziness, or haste.... The very purpose of science is to help us understand the complex world around us through simple explanations. The purpose of technology is to make new artifacts fulfill the needs of humans, not to make their lives more complicated. Our ancient human traits will ensure that we will only tolerate so much complexity; if the technologies of the Information Marketplace become too complex, we won't use them often and may just ignore them altogether.

—M. Dertouzos

INTRODUCTION

This chapter is concerned with giving us a solid understanding of the concept of cognitive complexity and how we can use the idea of managing cognitive complexity to develop LCD guidelines and evaluation schemes. In our context of interactive-information-field design (product, workspace, and information design), *cognitive complexity* (CC) refers to external elements that contribute directly to our neural load, thereby reducing our capacity to think clearly and understand: CC in our design context is the sum of those external factors which make things hard to see and use, hard to grasp, hard to understand. However specifically defined, the meaning of this term can still be a bit ambiguous, and many causes of CC or cognitive confusion (from mental illness to lack of proper nutrition) are beyond the scope of this work. Like *information, complexity* is a term much in vogue today and it has a multiplicity of meanings in a variety of different disciplines and contexts. So before we proceed to a detailed look at cognitive complexity per se, let us review (in a nontechnical manner) the dominant uses of the term by those disciplines that claim to directly concern themselves with complexity: systems theory and chaos theory. First, let us look at how the base concept, complexity itself, is defined in its common usage.

COMPLEX, COMPLICATED, AND COMPLEXITY

Reference sources from *Random House* (Stein, 1982) to *Webster's* (Gove, 1986) describe *complex, complicated,* or *complexity* in virtually the same terms, all making the connection between complexity and something difficult to understand. They also singularly portray the aspect of this "difficulty" as involving the arrangement or the organization of the parts of something in such a way that the individual parts or the relationships between them cannot be easily discerned or analyzed. Taking this definition as a link to other research, we can explore the interaction between LCD and complexity management. If we are interested in scaffolding (facilitating the learning process in LCD), we must ultimately make each of the parts (within an information-field) overtly evident and take the implicit relationships between these parts and make them explicit. This reinforces the contention that LCD needs to deal with sheer number, variety, interrelatedness, and hidden details found in the world if it is going to facilitate understanding. By augmenting the capacity of our own thinking and perception, LCD takes the natural complexity of number, variety, interrelatedness, and hidden details found in information-fields (people interrelated with products, information, workspaces) and organizes them in such a way that they are cognitively simplified and more easily understood. We will add extensive detail to this simplification process (as the antidote to complexification) as we move through the cognitive hierarchy in Chapters 4 through 10. Now to a quick look at systems and chaos theory.

COMPLEXITY AND THE FOUNDATIONS OF THE FUTURE OF DESIGN

Complexity as a research concept suffers from what a cognitive anthropologist might call the effect of the "hidden category." If asked to classify pets, an individual might very possibly list collies, dobermans, boxers, German shepherds, or springer spaniels without ever thinking of listing *dog*. The "hidden class" of dogs is lost in the list of actual breeds. Similarly, much that is complex is not spoken of as a complexity problem or in terms of the characteristics of complexity but is spoken of as information overload or misleading design or caused by rapid change. In a sense, we are missing the forest for the trees. Thus, our research emphasis has been placed on how we can deal with the information explosion or how we can improve poor design but not on how we can deal with complexity per se, to the net effect that our solutions have remained partial. Part of this book's aim is to raise our intellectual awareness of the power of "managing complexity" as an organizing concept that can help to stimulate the redesign of our interactive information-fields (I-FS) toward simplicity.

Not all disciplines have avoided complexity as a topic. Two areas of interrelated scholarship have taken direct aim at managing complexity in their own specialized context: systems theory and complexity theory.

Systems Theory and Design

The systems movement begun by von Bertalanffy and Weiner in the 1940s had as its initial target a way of thinking about complex natural objects, such as those found in biology, that would not attempt to simplify complexity in order to understand it but would instead understand complexity in order to simplify it. So, as opposed to the analytical reductionism of the scientific method, systems theory developed a vocabulary and method for describing the properties of wholes as wholes and focusing on the importance of internal and external relationships. It is within this movement that we get the well-known definition of a system as a whole that is greater than the sum of its parts. For an excellent description of the essential concepts and vocabulary of systems theory (which is beyond the scope of my effort here), I refer you to *General Systems Theory* by von Bertalanffy (1968) and *The Fifth Discipline* by Senge (1990). Still, from this brief backdrop we can see that the focus of complexity for systems thinkers has to do with the characteristics of wholeness and feedback, along with the numbers of parts and number of relationships involved in the system (see Flood & Carson's characterization in *Dealing With Complexity*, 1990, for further confirmation). Yates (1978) added to this the complexity-creating element of the lack of constraints; for Checkland (1981), complexity and systems theory merged in the confluence of a variety of concepts including emergence, communication and control, and hierarchy. "Together these contribute significantly to complexity, as when they are present, analysis becomes that much more difficult" (p. 28). Some distinctions to these basic tenets take the form of three *ranges* of complexity: "organized simplicity, organized complexity, and disorganized complexity" (p. 31). *Organized simplicity* occurs when a small number of significant factors is buried in a large number of insignificant factors, *disorganized complexity* occurs when the system contains a large number of variables that behave randomly, and *organized complexity* describes systems that are rich, purposeful, and relational. It is organized complexity that we will be dealing with in LCD, as it includes understanding the needs and expectations of customers, as well as their cognitive makeup.

Senge (1990) wrote in *The Fifth Discipline* of two types of system complexity found in organizations: detail and dynamic. *Detail complexity* is the kind of complexity characterized by a multiplicity of variables, and it is handled by the sophisticated tools of forecasting, business analysis, and elegant strategic planning. Senge described the equally important, yet more elusive concept of *dynamic complexity* as resulting "when the same action has dramatically different effects in the short run and the long run,... when an action has one set of consequences locally and a very different set of consequences in another part of the system, ... when obvious interventions produce non-obvious consequences" (p. 71). Both detail and dynamic complexity must be dealt with in any successful LCD approach because we are dealing with the need to support understanding. And understanding today requires dealing with many details and dealing with the dynamic hyperlinked nature of human thought embedded in a global economy.

Many design-related lessons can be gleaned from the study of systems and its perspective on complexity. This is because systems thinking was invented specifically as a mode of thinking capable of penetrating complex organizations of objects and relationships (like sending an astronaut to the moon and back). It is exactly the growing complexity of parts and their interrelationships that plagues our designs of products, information, and workspaces (I-FS). All this being said, the key lesson to be derived from systems thinking is that even though our perception of things may seem to focus on the limited parts of an interaction with an object, our minds will also seek to understand the product or information design as a whole and in doing so will form a distributed connection between itself and the artifact—a connection I have called an information-field. Thus, somewhere in our design there must be a coherency that makes sense, or helps us to make sense, of all the relationships that cause the entire user-object interaction to be greater than the sum of the parts.

Complexity Science and Design

What does complexity science add to our everyday understanding of the characteristics of complexity? If we look at the development of thought over time from Laszlo's (1987) *Evolution: The Grand Synthesis* through Nicolis and Prigogine's *Exploring Complexity* (1989) and Goerner's (1990) essay on chaos theory to Cohen and Stewart's *Collapse of Chaos* (1994), we see a consistent theme: Because of high rates of interaction, simple causes can create complex effects. That is, from simple components, like the four nucleotides of DNA and a simple set of rules governing how they can interact, we can get an almost infinite variety of complex life forms.

Goerner's (1990) essay on chaos theory, delineated the five characteristics that make complex systems complex: (a) variable reactivity, (b) codeterminism, (c) coupling, (d) coherence, and (e) iteration. Variable reactivity or the sensitivity of a system to small differences is the "most fundamental characteristic of complexity" (p. 436). This hypersensitivity means that small differences can have large effects and large differences can have small effects. Codeterminism or interactionism means that elements within different systems can mutually affect one another and may even reciprocally determine the function of the other system in an ongoing way that produces order. The principle of coupling or connectivity states that two unstable systems can join to form a higher-level system that is itself stable. That is, simple subsystems give rise to more complex systems and thus form the basis of the evolution of systems over time. Coherency or "hidden order" means that complex systems, even though they may seem chaotic, are actually orderly. Thus,

> Whether we conceive of it as coming from codeterminism, coupling, or simply non-linearity, one major new understanding of complexity is that in bumping around, things don't just get diffused; they can also come to cohere into systems. Complexity does not result in a billiard ball universe but a universe of coherent processes. (p. 439)

Complex systems do not fall into simple repetitive states but are iteratively incorporating their environments to produce infinitely unique behaviors that never repeat. Lastly, Goerner noted that the five cornerstones of complexity listed above are also fundamental notions of existing enterprises such as ecology and pointed out that the same intricate sensitivity and connectivity is often described by ecologists of their domain.

This description of complexity reminds us of Senge's "dynamic complexity" and goes a long way in proposing a rationale for the existence of that kind of complication in organizations and human endeavors of all sorts. It also explains why good design is so difficult to achieve. In addition to the focus on wholeness and relationship in systems theory and systems thinking, complexity science says that to truly understand something we must understand how it will change over time. The good news about change is that the dynamic nature of things can eventually lead to models that are more complex yet can be understood more easily because of their higher degree of integrated wholeness. The lesson for designers, then, is to keep in mind that even though there seems to be many complicated product elements or a lot of information to organize or information flowing through a workspace, there is an underlying emergent simplicity or whole that can be identified and relied on to provide a basis for coherent design even in the midst of dynamic change.

Other Usages of Cognitive Complexity

A few other research efforts have used the specific term *cognitive complexity.* To clarify my usage in the upcoming sections, I will briefly distinguish my concept of cc from two other popular uses of the term.

Kieras and Polson (1985) were perhaps the first to use the term *cognitive complexity* in their work. They proposed a quantitative model for the amount of knowledge required in a knowledge structure (GOMS) for the individual to understand how to perform a task such as word processing. This was called the CCT or the cognitive complexity model. More specifically, they identified cognitive complexity as a measure of the number of production rules it would take to implement the methods and control structures described in the GOMS (goals, operators, methods, and selection) model (developed by Card, Moran, & Newell, 1983) to perform any particular task. My cc model is qualitative and not quantitative, but it does not conflict with the notion that complexity adds a neural load to learning any task. Also, not being quantitative, my use of cc is more concerned with managing complexity in large chunks than with measuring its internal effects.

Ceci and Ruiz (1992), in studying our ability to generalize and the transfer of skills, defined *cognitive complexity* as the ability to integrate differentiated facts into functional insights within or across domains. Their review concluded that transfer across domains or even within domains was relatively rare and not dependent on IQ. For our design context cc is not a skill in handling complexity but characteristics of users and objects, information, and environments (I-FS) that make understanding and skill transfer less likely to occur.

Now that we have explored and linked the idea of complexity to our idea of understanding and have clarified other uses of the term cognitive complexity, we have a good basis on which to take a new look at cognitive complexity, a look that will lead us to LCD guidelines and LCD evaluation methods.

COGNITIVE COMPLEXITY

Cognitive complexity (cc) is a form of complexity that has some of the characteristics of other conceptualizations of complexity but is essentially different in context. Rather than focusing on the abstract basis of complex systems, I plan to focus on the concrete factors in our environment that assault our everyday postindustrial lives, increasing our neural load and making it difficult for us to function effectively in the learning, problem-solving, and decision-making aspects of our lives. This conceptualization of cc within our design context is developed below.

Five Major Sources

To explain cc in some detail, I will first list the major sources of cc, then provide brief descriptions of each of these sources along with an associated set of antonyms or *word-pairs*.

The major sources of cc are as follows:

1. Metasocial forces (Bell, 1973; Gergen, 1991; Toffler, 1970)
2. Information overload (Klapp, 1986; Toffler, 1970; Wurman, 1989)
3. Complex problems (Voss, Wolfe, Lawrence, & Engle, 1991)
4. System complexity (Flood & Carson, 1990)
5. Incoherent design (Norman, 1988)

General Form of the Word-Pairs

Each word-pair is made up of complex-versus-simple antonyms. In general, the more complex end of the pair is shown on the left, and the simpler, less complex end of the pair appears on the right, as shown in Table 2.1. The word-pairs are meant to clarify and accentuate some of the critical characteristics of each of the sources.

Table 2.1. Some Complexity Pairs

Complexifying	Simplifying
Ill structured	Structured
Novelty	Confirmation
Hidden	Apparent

Metasocial Forces and Information Overload

I will present the first two sets of word-pairs together because information overload and metasocial forces are very closely aligned. The metasocial forces of complexity are (a) dynamic rates of change and the constant introduction of novelty and (b) the sheer volume of possible interactions people have with each other, products, and information. Information is the substrate that drives these forces because it is the source of new knowledge, and new knowledge creates novelty. Information and knowledge are together the fuel of social evolution:

Thus, information is the axis around which an understanding of the systemic picture of complexity circles. The outward signs of complexity, seen in the evolution of society, are fueled by the storage, development, and transmission of information. As more information is produced, stored and distributed in our society the more complex society becomes. Yet, as more information is made available for use by the members of society the more new information they, in turn, are able to produce. (Reeves, 1996, pp. 29–30)

This *spiraling complexification* causes endless rounds of change and endless feelings of falling behind under a heavier and more formidable neural load.

Metasocial Forces Word-Pairs

Table 2.2 lists some of the word-pairs for metasocial forces as a source of complexity. These pairs are based on change, interactions, and the contraction of time.

Table 2.2.   Word-Pairs for Metasocial Forces

Complexifying	Simplifying
Novelty (new)	Confirmation (same)
Dynamic (constant change)	Stable (changeless)
Variety (many choices)	Redundancy (few choices)
Hurried (unplanned)	Thought Out (planned)

Information Overload Word-Pairs

Information-based complexity, as experienced by an individual, may be described by the following pairs of antonyms: *order* and *disorder, confirmation* and *novelty, redundancy* and *variety, signal* and *noise, differentiated* and *undifferentiated,* and *negentropy* and *entropy.* It is important to note that these pairs do not carry a sense of positive or negative or good or bad but measure the relative simplicity or complexity of that being rated. For example, if we are evaluating the design of the weather page of USA *Today* we can check either end on the pairs of antonyms that we think applies to that information design. This rating again aims at only our evaluation of the complexity that we experience in interacting with the page. As an example of how these information-based complexity pairs were created, let us look at Klapp's (1986) analysis of redundancy and variety. Klapp separated redundancy and variety into two main categories, dividing "good" and "boring" versions of each into four quadrants. Good or functional redundancy includes things like rules, skills, and codes. Boring and banal redundancy consists of platitudes, tedium, dogmatism, cliches, restriction, and monotony. Good variety consists of discovery, learning, and invention. Boring variety includes noise, ambiguity, trivia, and irrelevance. Klapp's important analysis shows us that simplicity alone cannot be the target of LCD because it can include elements of banality that are not useful to learning. So as we proceed into the development of the design guidelines using these word-pairs, we need to keep in mind the usefulness of CC as a design approach but remember that it will be necessary, in optimizing design solutions, to find a balance between unnecessary complexification and unnecessary and banal simplicity.

Table 2.3 lists the word-pairs for information overload as a source of complexity.

Table 2.3.   Word-Pairs for Information Overload

Complexifying	Simplifying
Disorder (uncategorized)	Order (categorized)
Novelty (new)	Confirmation (known)
Variety (inconsistent)	Redundancy (consistent)
Noise (irrelevant)	Signal (relevant)
Undifferentiated (indistinct)	Differentiated (distinct)

Complex Problem Solving

Problem solving came into its own at midcentury with the combination of Polya's (1985) work on heuristics and Newell and Simon's (1972) work on human problem solving. Within their information-processing approach, problem solving is defined as a process of search through the decision space looking for the right "operator" to transform the problem "space" into a solution (see Chapter 5). Complex problems are those that require a more difficult search through a more complicated maze of possible operators. Complexity, then, is a matter of the difficulty in finding the right operators that will eventually lead to the ultimate solution. For Voss et al. (1991), the characteristics of complexity in problem solving include the specificity and structuredness of the goal representation and the pressure of the importance of the decision (which could include time and consequences pressure): for example, the Cuban missile crisis, or testimony before a grand jury. Ill-structured complex problems have vague goals, a lack of constraints, and perhaps no known method of achieving a solution. Lesgold and Lajoie (1991) studied problem solving in their work on expertise in electronics. Experts differ from novices in the amount of domain specific knowledge they have and how that knowledge is chunked or categorized (see Chapter 9). "Experts have more memory for information involved in the solution of a problem, and thus better memory retrieval and pattern recognition to specific domains" (p. 289). In a study of expertise in electronics troubleshooting, they reported: (a) Experts use many observations in a sequence of simple decisions; (b) the goal is the search for the faulty component; (c) experts use hierarchically embedded representations of the problem; and (d) "search is very opportunistic, with switches between recognition, topographical search, symptom-tracing procedures and functional analysis procedures" (p. 291), depending on the information available.

Funke (1991) described complex problem solving by contrasting it to non-complex problem solving. This works well for creating pairs of antonyms. His list is also very cognitively oriented. Funke's list of simplifying elements includes

1. Availability of information about the problem

2. Precision of goal definition

3. A reduced number of variables, degrees of connectivity, and the linear relationships between them

4. The stability of the properties of the problem or time dependencies in the course of the problem-solving process

So complex problem solving is made of the opposite characteristics:

1. *Intransparency:* Only some variables lend themselves to direct observation. "Often, only knowledge about 'symptoms' is available from which one has to infer the underlying state.... Other cases of intransparency arise if variables can be assessed in principle, but their huge number requires selection of a few relevant ones" (p. 186).

2. *Multiple goals:* With multiple goals some may be contradictory, and trade-offs are often required.

3. *Complexity of the situation:* This may conflict with the limited capacity of the problem solver to think it through. (Funke's *complexity* is similar to the definitions of complexity I listed above. It is not just the number

of variables but how they can interact and whether or not they can be controlled).

4. *Connectivity:* Complex problems often contain a high degree of connectivity or interrelationship; In other words, it is very difficult to anticipate all the possible consequences of a given situation.

5. *The dynamic nature of complex problems:* In other words, complex problems can worsen, creating great time pressure and unpredictability.

6. *Time delay:* In complex problems, there can be a delay between the action taken and the response or the appearance of consequences. This places an extra burden on the problem solver.

Complex Problem-Solving Word-Pairs

Table 2.4 lists the word-pairs for problem solving as a source of complexity.

Table 2.4. Word-Pairs for Problem Solving

Complexifying	Simplifying
High number of variables (hard to track)	Few variables (easy to track)
Hidden (murky details)	Apparent (clarity of fact)
Expert (expertise required)	Novice (beginner can do)
Many solutions (possibly contradictory)	One solution (no conflict)
Vagueness of goal (indeterminate)	Specificity of goal (singular goal)
Ill structured (lack of organization)	Structured (organized)
Interactive subsystems (hidden effects)	Singular subsystems (expected effects)
Nonlinear (unpredictable)	Linear (predictable)
Illogical (random)	Logical (ordered)
Unpredictable (cannot find cause)	Predictable (can find cause)
Time delayed (unknown effect)	Immediate (known effect)

Design Complexity

The study of cognitive complexity in visual and object design has been spearheaded by the work of Donald Norman, Alan Kay, Doug Engelbart, and Jacob Nielsen. In *User Centered System Design* (Norman & Draper, 1986) and *The Psychology of Everyday Things* (Norman, 1988), Norman and others have set out many of the critical characteristics that would reduce the complexity of interacting with an interface. In his latter work, Norman's object of design is especially applicable to our own interest in cc. His focus on the elements of everyday design fits with my broadened scope of the objects that need to be carefully designed, moving beyond computer-based learning systems to products, information, and workspaces. His discussion of good design principles can be used to help construct our design-based complexity word-pairs.

From Norman's (1988) list of "good" design principles, we can deduce the following elements of complexity:

1. Not enough information is supplied to build an adequate mental model.
2. Tasks require extensive use of memory and/or problem-solving skills.
3. There are no mental aids.
4. There is no visual feedback on the results of an action.
5. There is a lack of a visual display of what actions are possible.
6. There is response incompatibility with the user's expectations.
7. Lack of constraints allows the user choices between too many options.
8. There is no flexibility to allow for error.
9. There are no standards.

To this list I want to add the complexity-causing effects of designed-in barriers, from physical barriers to the disabled to the process barriers constructed within bureaucracies.

Nielsen and Molich's (1990) article on heuristic evaluation methods lists six "heuristics" that enhance the usability of interfaces and adds to our model of cognitive complexity. Their classic usability issues are (a) the use of natural dialogue, (b) using terms familiar to the expected audience, (c) minimizing need for memory, (d) being consistent in all aspects, (e) always providing feedback, (f) using methods like constraint to avoid errors, (g) clearly marking exits, and (h) providing shortcuts. From Nielsen's and Norman's models, we can construct our antonym word-pairs.

Design Word-Pairs

Table 2.5 lists the word-pairs for design as a source of complexity.

Table 2.5. Word-Pairs for Design

Complexifying	Simplifying
Inhumane (machine centered)	Humane (human centered)
Hidden (guessed next action)	Apparent (known next action)
No help (not available)	Help (available)
Nonstandard (inconsistent)	Standard (consistent)
Textual (high neural load)	Graphic (low neural load)
Illogical (high neural load)	Logical (low neural load)
Obscure (difficult to identify)	Obvious (easy to identify)
Unbounded (many choices)	Constrained (one choice)
Large/long tasks (error-prone)	Small/brief tasks (error-free)
Single method (constrained)	Shortcuts (adaptable)
Unnatural (unexpected result)	Natural (expected result)

Systems Complexity

As mentioned above in our description of systems theory, system scientists (Banathy, 1991; Flood & Carson, 1990) have developed a conceptualization of systems complexity described as existing when at least one of the following system attributes is found:

1. Significant interactions
2. High numbers of parts
3. Nonlinearity
4. Broken symmetry
5. Lack of constraints
6. Open versus closed to their environment

7. Human versus machine

8. Emergence—characteristics of a whole different from any of its parts

Systems Complexity Word-Pairs

Table 2.6 lists the word-pairs for systems as a source of complexity.

Table 2.6. Word-Pairs for Systems Complexity

Complexifying	Simplifying
Interactive subsystems (many interactions)	Singular relationships (few interactions)
Many parts (unconstrained interactions)	Few parts (constrained)
Dynamic behavior (unpredictable)	Linear behavior (predictable)
Open (reacts with environs)	Closed (self-contained)
Broken symmetry (fluctuations)	Symmetry (homeostasis)
Differentiated (specialized)	Undifferentiated (unspecialized)
Soft systems (human)	Hard systems (mechanical)
Human activity systems (unpredictable)	Mechanical systems (predictable)
Anarchic (no control mechanism)	Communications/control (feedback control)
Embedded (hidden interactions)	Single (obvious interactions)

Overlapping Word-Pairs

For our purposes, it is important to note that some of the word-pairs are repeated in multiple sources: That is, identical characteristics describe different sources of complexity. This is important because in our efforts to manage complexity, we are really aiming at managing the characteristics described by the word-pairs. The number of unique pairs may actually be smaller if we take all the sources together and treat them as a whole. As much as this can be done, we can reduce the scope of our management effort. I do, however, believe that in order to manage complexity adequately, we must manage the contributions from all of its sources. The overlapping pairs to be considered are listed below:

1. Between metasocial forces and information overload
   - Novelty/Confirmation
   - Variety/Redundancy
2. Between complex problem solving and design
   - Hidden/Apparent
   - Illogical/Logical
3. Between complex problem solving and systems
   - Many solutions/One solution
   - Interactive subsystems/Singular relationships
   - Dynamic/Linear

CONCLUSION

In this chapter, we have begun the process of creating effective LCD criteria based on facilitating learning; because any LCD scheme must ultimately resolve the question of how understanding is to be gained in an environment of increasing complexity and neural load. We have set out in this chapter to describe cognitive complexity (CC) to such a level of detail that we can develop design guidelines for LCD and modify heuristic evaluation methods to include the management of complexity as a legitimate and useful design criterion. To this end, I have described the major origins of CC and have broken those sources down into characteristics identified by word-pairs that have then been further described with short explanatory phrases. We are now ready to look at design evaluation schemes based on word-pairs and construct a LCD scheme for evaluating cognitive complexity in consumer products, information delivery systems of all sorts, and workspaces. This is the task of Chapter 3.

3
Evaluating Cognitive Complexity

> Cognitive tools, on the whole, are information-based tools, ones with interior representations and for which the design problems are complex. There is no folk design for cognitive artifacts. ... Cognitive tools are simply harder to get right.
>
> —Donald Norman

The design of "cognitive tools" *is* harder to get right! This chapter is about creating a unique set of evaluation methods capable of measuring the effectiveness of LCD in order to get it right. As we move through the chapters of Part II, we will elicit a series of design principles, some quite old, others new, based on some aspect of research in cognitive or information science that specifically attacks cognitive complexity (CC). Some of the guidelines will help manage complexity by aligning with known laws of perception, some with the power of visualization, and yet others with an understanding of how categorization works or how mental models naturally form themselves into web-like networks. From this analysis, I will create three LCD evaluation tools. Toward this purpose, we will also briefly review some recent work done in the development of quick and inexpensive computer interface evaluation techniques (Nielsen, 1992), looking for examples of techniques that can serve as models for our tools. Note that even though we are looking at *interface* evaluation techniques in this case, they are appropriate to our more general design audience because LCD always considers all user-product interaction as an interaction seeking understanding at the point of an interface. In other words, *all* products have "interfaces," and their designs should be cognitively sound. It is also helpful to use these methods as models because they have been shown, through extensive testing, to be very effective at what they are specifically targeted to do. Specifically, we are going to look at some examples of quick usability inspection methods that use either human-computer interface (HCI) experts or the interface designers themselves to test the design—for example, heuristic evaluation and cognitive walk-throughs (Jefferies, Miller, Wharton, & Uyeda, 1991; Nielsen, 1992; Treu, 1994). We will also employ a word-scale scheme after Guillemette (1989).

DEVELOPMENT OF A COMPLEXITY
EVALUATION SCHEME

One of the goals of this book is to produce proposals for three different adjunct evaluation tools that can be useful in LCD:

1. Word-pair complexity rating scales
2. A questionnaire focused on content
3. A checklist of design principles

Nielsen's heuristic evaluation scheme will be the model for the checklist of design principles. The cognitive walk-through strategy will be the model for the questionnaire, and Guillemettes's semantic scale will be the model for our word-pair scales scheme. In this chapter, I will create the word-scales, but the other tools will be created after we have gone through the cognitive hierarchy of Chapters 4 through 10. So let us proceed with a brief introduction to these evaluation methods.

Heuristic Evaluation (Nielsen & Molich, 1990)

According to Nielsen and Molich, there are four classes of usability evaluation: formal, automatic, empirical, and heuristic. Formal and automatic forms of evaluation have yet to reach the stage where they can be applied, and the most widely used, the empirical, is time consuming and costly. With this up-front cost, most developers cannot afford to carry out empirical studies. Thus, there has been a call for some form of evaluation that is quick and inexpensive, yet results in the same quality of final design. This is where Nielsen's work on heuristic design has come to be applied. The heuristic class of usability evaluation is growing in popularity because it is inexpensive, is intuitive, does not require much advanced planning, and is rated as being pretty effective (especially in groups).

Heuristic evaluation is an informal process of passing judgment according to HCI expert opinion. An individual or group of HCI experts can carry out in-depth analyses of interface designs to isolate those features that may cause problems in usability. Also, to balance the informality of the review, the inspection process should include written heuristics to guide the evaluators

(Treu, 1994). This method, when carried out by experts, was found to be the most effective in finding serious usability flaws. An example of a classic interface usability heuristic is the following:

- Include simple and natural dialogue.
- Speak in the user's language.
- Minimize user memory load.
- Be consistent.
- Provide user feedback.
- Prevent errors.
- Provide clearly marked exits.
- Provide shortcuts.

This form of evaluation by inspection relies on a written heuristic to guide the reviewers. The LCD guidelines checklist will be modeled after this method.

Cognitive Walk-Through (Jeffries et al., 1991)

This method is based on a walk-through of the interface being designed in the context of the core tasks faced by the user. The walk-through is performed by the designer. The actions and feedback of the system are compared to the user's expected goals and knowledge, and any discrepancies between them can be modified. We can extend that concept of carefully focusing on user expectation and domain knowledge to include issues dealing with content and understandability. This would include issues of how the information-field is meeting the content needs of the user in accordance with his or her information-seeking requirements, performance goals, and level of familiarity with the topics encountered. We can use this method to inspire the creation of our content-understandability questionnaire.

Semantic-Differential Scale (Guillemette, 1989)

Table 3.1 is an example of scales developed by Guillemette to determine the readability of documentation.

Table 3.1.   Guillemette's Semantic-Differential Scales for Document Readability

Concept Chunk	Semantic Scale							
Credibility	Correct							Incorrect
		1	2	3	4	5	6	7
Fitness	Relevant							Extraneous
		1	2	3	4	5	6	7
Systematic arrangement	Organized							Unorganized
		1	2	3	4	5	6	7
	Structured							Unstructured
		1	2	3	4	5	6	7
	Orderly							Chaotic
		1	2	3	4	5	6	7
Understandability	Clear							Confusing
		1	2	3	4	5	6	7
	Understandable							Mysterious
		1	2	3	4	5	6	7

The beauty of the use of scales is that they are quick and easy to fill out and score. The primary challenge of the scales scheme is in finding relevant terms to describe the aspects of the system that one wishes to operationalize. In text understanding, the relevant aspects are correctness, relevance, organization, and so on. Secondarily, as Guillemette's example shows, it is helpful to categorize these "relevant aspects" or chunk them under larger defining concepts. For readability, Guillemette used defining concepts such as credibility, fitness, systematic arrangement, and so on. In developing our LCD scale (see Table 3.2), I use the complexity word-pairs (combined with a 1 through 7 rating) as the relevant words to score and the five "sources" of cognitive complexity as the chunking or classifying concepts. Thus, this is the perfect method for developing our word-pair scales. In the next section, I will combine the word-pairs from Chapter 2 with the rating scales of Guillemette and create our first evaluation tool.

WORD-SCALE SCHEME FOR COGNITIVE COMPLEXITY

In this section, we convert the complexity word-pairs into general-purpose scales that have the ability to rate the complexity management achieved in the design of a wide variety of interactive-information-fields (I-FS)—from interfaces to indices, from catalogues to curriculum modules, from classification systems to visualization schemes, from appliances to workspace elements. It is interesting to note that the heuristic elements of usability testing listed by Nielsen and Molich (1990) above can be extrapolated to many of the elements of our complexity scales, reconfirming that in managing the usability of the hci we are involved at a very basic level with managing the general complexity of all I-F interactions.

Table 3.2 is a rating scale after Guillemette (1989), drawn from a selected portion of the complexity word-pairs of Chapter 2. It lists a series of scales that can be marked by evaluators of any particular I-F design. I am using the complexity sources themselves (metasocial forces, information overload, systems, design, and complex problems) as the organizing chunks for the sets of relevant aspects. For purposes of conciseness and manageability I am using only a representative subset of all the word-pairs possible. For explanatory phrases describing each of the antonyms, please refer back to the original word-pairs in Chapter 2.

Table 3.2. Origins and Elements of Complexity

Origin	Elements of Complexity						
	Novelty						Confirmation
	7	6	5	4	3	2	1
	Dynamic						Stable
	7	6	5	4	3	2	1
Metasocial Forces and Information Overload	Variety						Redundancy
	7	6	5	4	3	2	1
	Disorder						Order
	7	6	5	4	3	2	1
	Noise						Signal
	7	6	5	4	3	2	1

Table 3.2. Origins and Elements of Complexity *(Continued)*

Origin	Elements of Complexity						
Systems	Interactive						Singular
	7	6	5	4	3	2	1
	Many						One
	7	6	5	4	3	2	1
	Circular						Linear
	7	6	5	4	3	2	1
	Broken Symmetry						Symmetry
	7	6	5	4	3	2	1
Design	Approximate						Precise
	7	6	5	4	3	2	1
	Hidden						Apparent
	7	6	5	4	3	2	1
	Nonstandardized						Standardized
	7	6	5	4	3	2	1
	Illogical						Logical
	7	6	5	4	3	2	1
	Obscure						Obvious
	7	6	5	4	3	2	1
	Unbounded						Constrained
	7	6	5	4	3	2	1
Problem Solving	Expert						Novice
	7	6	5	4	3	2	1
	Unstructured						Structured
	7	6	5	4	3	2	1
	Many Solutions						One Solution
	7	6	5	4	3	2	1

CONCLUSION

This is the Age of Complexity: a period of escalating growth in the cognitive load on human performance, understanding, decision making, and problem solving. Design as a profession carries a responsibility for its role in this explosion of complexity. What can designers do to help alleviate the problems brought on by increasing complexity? I have proposed that a LCD scheme, if applied broadly, could have a significant impact on complexity by facilitating understanding and lifting consumer confidence. To this end, I have created a method for organizing the characteristics of cognitive complexity and have created an evaluation tool based on this organization. Two other guidelines have also been proposed:

1. A questionnaire that will guide reviewers in analyzing information-fields in terms of the adequacy of content. This means that we not only look at the organization of information but, like instructors, also evaluate the content for its ability to scaffold understanding in its users.

2. A structured checklist of design guidelines

LOOKING AHEAD

In Part II, I will examine many of the foundational topics of the cognitive sciences, such as perception, categorization, and representation, along with their corresponding manifestations in the information sciences, such as interface design, classification systems, and hypertext navigation. In this process, we will move up the entire cognitive hierarchy from the lower-level cognitive functions to higher-order thinking and collaboration. In doing this, I have given chapters, such titles as "Learner as Perceiver," "Learner as Problem Solver," and "Learner as Model Builder" to emphasize the effect on, and responsibility toward, learning that each cognitive function can provide. It is necessary to cover the higher spectrum of what we know about human cognition because LCD needs to be as concerned with scaffolding under-standing, and supporting visualization, as it is in using the correct Gestalt principles. At the end of each chapter I will first map the chapter's component of cognitive research to the word-pair scales in order to detect any applicability it may have in attacking the problem of managing complexity for learners. Then we will see how specific research points can be used to construct our other evaluative goals: the design checklist and the content questionnaire. Chapter 4 begins the process of looking at relevant cognitive and information science research, starting with the basics of perception, Gestalt, information design, and the essence of making a good abstract. Table 3.3 lists the topical focus of Chapters 4 through 9. The topics in these chapters are so interrelated that it quickly becomes apparent that the divisions of subject material from one chapter to the next are artificial. For example, in problem solving we have elements of perception, search, mental models, and expertise. In the topic of hypertext, there are also concerns for perception, search, classification, relevance, learning, and expertise. This overlap speaks to the complex nature of the discussed topics and is why I have chosen to form an explicit interdisciplinary link between the cognitive and information sciences.

Table 3.3. Topics of Chapters 4 through 9

Chapter Title	Cognitive Science	Information Science
4. Learner as Perceiver	Gestalt/Perception	Information Design & Abstracts
5. Learner as Model Builder	Problem Solving and Representation	Cognitive Engineering and Hypertext Information
6. Learner as Categorizer	Categorization	Classification
7. Learner as Searcher	Visualization	Direct Manipulation and DQI and Information Seeking
8. Learner as Expert	Expertise/Heuristics	Knowledge Engineering
9. Learner as Student	Schema-based Instruction and Thinking Modes	Computer-based LCD Software Design

PART II.
Managing Complexity

4

Learner as Perceiver

In 1888 Emile Bernard, whose ideas would seriously influence ... the whole of modern art, decided that the painter should not paint things but the idea of a thing. ... If you paint from memory instead of from objects, ... you can rid yourself of the useless complication of shapes and shades. All you will get is a schematic presentation: all lines back to their geometric architecture, all shades back to the primary colors.... In search of simplification, it is necessary to seek the origins of everything, in pure color, and in geometry which provided the typical form of all objective forms.

—E. Weber

ABOUT THIS CHAPTER

The LCD focus of this chapter is on issues of perception for learners. This chapter includes discussions and examples from

- Cognitive science on Gestalt perception principles

- Information science on information design, interface design, and creating abstracts

The resulting design principles are extracted and listed at the end of the chapter.

As an organizational reminder to the reader, the above pattern of presentation will be repeated in the upcoming Chapters 5 through 9. See Table 4.1. That is, we will highlight a particular view of the learner as perceiver, model builder, searcher, and so on, first with relevant research from the cognitive sciences and then with associated research from the information sciences.

Table 4.1. Developing the LCD Tools

LCD Discovery Process	Moving through Layers of the Cognitive Hierarchy—Identifying Design Principles					
	Chapter 4 — Perception Principles	Chapter 5 — Mental Model	Chapter 6 — Categorization	Chapter 7 — Visualization	Chapter 8 — Expertise	Chapter 9 — Learning
Extracting Design Principles for Dealing with Increasingly Higher Levels of Interactive Complexity — Product Perspective Only / Interactive-Information-Field Individual Perspective / Interactive-Information-Field Collaborative Perspective	Design principles drawn from this layer of the hierarchy	Design principles drawn from this layer of the hierarchy	Design principles drawn from this layer of the hierarchy	Design principles drawn from this layer of the hierarchy	Design principles drawn from this layer of the hierarchy	Design principles drawn from this layer of the hierarchy

In this manual, we will follow the process of extracting design principles as we move up the human cognitive hierarchy, from basic perception to creative problem solving. As we move through this hierarchy, we will focus on those cognitive strategies that help us to manage complexity. In Chapter 10, we summarize the principles in the LCD *tool kit.*

INTRODUCTION

In our search for a general methodology of simplification—that is, the management of complexity in information-field (product, information, or workspace) design—we are first going to look at that vital intersection between learners and the knowledge they seek to acquire: the interface. The interface can be a gateway to learning or a severe barrier. Moran defined the user interface as consisting of those aspects of the product, system, or space that the user comes into contact with physically, perceptually, and conceptually (cited in Farooq & Dominick, 1988). This chapter explores the perceptual responsiveness of an information-field that occurs at its interface as users, whether professionals or students, try to interact with it. Our purpose in this inquiry is to clarify the use of perceptual elements in LCD. Chapter 5 will continue beyond the perceptual level of LCD to the conceptual notion of the interface based on the development of several cognitive models the designer's model, the user's model, and the systems model.

It is important to remember that we are defining *interface* and *interactive information-field* in a very broad sense, from a teacher-curriculum-classroom situation, to a newspaper, to the surfaces of products or the furniture and integrated tool components of a workspace, to interfaces on the World Wide Web, or a network computer attached to an intranet.

The theme of this chapter and the next is that the interaction between a user and an interface is cognitively equivalent to the organizational effects of both perception and action-oriented problem-solving strategies. Thus, to begin our discussion of the cognitive basis of interface design and, more broadly, information-field design, we will be reviewing perception and their Gestalt organization principles and the cognitive theories of problem solving (Chapter 5). In conjunction with the discussion of Gestalt principles, I will present a related information science perspective on perception with a review of the visual communication design principles of Wurman (1997), Tufte (1990), and Mullet and Sano (1995). In addition, we will explore the relationship between the art of creating abstracts in library and information science and the art of visual communication in interface design.

MANAGING COMPLEXITY FOR THE LEARNER AS PERCEIVER

Background: External Perception and Internal Images

Gardner (1985) described the history of the general debate and study of perception as beginning with the Greeks, when Democritus, Plato, and

Aristotle laid out the future course of investigation as either (a) understanding how we can so richly recognize objects in the world or (b) understanding the eye's anatomy and how the eye and sensory structures actually work. Continuing this dichotomy centuries later, Helmholtz believed that we needed to supplement perception with mental activity to understand what that we were looking at, whereas Gibson and the pure sensationalists believed that we picked up enough by simply perceiving our environment to make all the sense we needed of what we saw. It was their contention that "perception begins with the detection of elementary bits of sensation" (p. 296), out of which we build more complex wholes. The Gestaltists, following Helmholtz, asserted the opposite: that "one first perceives overall form" in a top-down fashion (inferring from preconceived notions) (p. 316). Today, in this dispute, the cognitivists, or those who favor perception plus inference, hold the dominant view over those who favor the direct perception theory (p. 316). The theory of how perception occurs is concomitant with the theory of how images are stored: that is, the theory of imagery and image representation. Analogous to perception, there are two competing perspectives on imagery as well: Either (a) there are special forms of internal mental models used to hold images (arguments of Kosslyn, 1996), or (b) images can be explained adequately in terms of the normal rule-based representations that describe other intellectual content. Today, this controversy is still unresolved. Now let us take a look at what we do know and how perception applies to design.

Within the framework of the overall LCD scheme of learnability, usability, and understandability, the elements and principles of perception most apply to, and are directed at, facilitating learnability and usability or competency in the use of the system, tool, or space. Following the principles of perception will not accomplish all the design goals of LCD, but they are still a necessary and important constituent of the total package.

Perception: Gestalt, Context, and Attention

When we recognize an object or detect the meaning of speech, we are recognizing a pattern. The essence of pattern recognition is found in the answer to the question, How do we decide to put certain features together in order to "form" a certain pattern? The answer lies in three elements of perception: the Gestalt principles of organization, attention, and context. The Gestalt (configuration) psychologists believed (a) that the key to understanding perception was to be found in studying the way the brain organizes basic stimuli and (b) that "organization of perception into patterns" is an inherent ability of humans (Solso, 1994, p. 89). In their research on the organization of perception, they identified the six principles discussed next.

Gestalt Concepts

Gestalt principles of organization begin with the basic premise that the whole is greater than the sum of the parts (systems). That is, people can and do recognize configurations in their entirety before they recognize the components of the perceived object. This basic principle is followed by the other Gestalt principles of proximity, similarity, good continuation, closure, and *Pragnanz*. In *Cognition and the Visual Arts*, Solso (1994) discussed each of these Gestalt elements in some detail.

Proximity. If "like objects are located near each other, ... we tend to group them together perceptually," or to put it another way, we tend to organize proximal stimuli (if they are similar in shape, color, or form) into patterns. In a multimedia age, it is well to note that proximity also works for graphics and music. In Solso's model of pattern recognition,

> The seeing of complex visual forms, as when we view art, is a matter of sensing basic shapes, passing them along to a receptive brain and combining the impression with our caste knowledge of the world from which inferences are fashioned. (p. 90)

Similarity. As we saw with proximity, it is the similar objects that tend to be grouped together, exposing our natural inclination to see similar elements as belonging to the same class. As with proximity, it is important to note that not having similarity, or having competing sets of similar elements, will cause a lack of coherent organization in the perceptual field and will limit the communicability of the information perceived there.

Continuation. Our eyes seem to "go with the flow" (p. 94). Objects that flow in one direction are likely to be seen as belonging together. "We see things in motion as, more or less, keeping on course rather than making oblique angular changes in midcourse" (p. 94).

Closure. As similarity is related to proximity, closure is related to continuation. Closure is the tendency to see figures as unitary or enclosed wholes. We add meaning to pieces or fragments and create a whole figure where there may be only an outline.

Pragnanz. This is the Gestalt principle that contends that our minds seek regular stable figures such as triangles or completed patterns in music. The psychological implication of *Pragnanz* is that without stability the viewer or listener will feel uneasy. Learning may require some feelings of unease or a sense of a "gap in what is needed," but too much perceptual instability will not perform the scaffolding function we are looking for with perceptual design cues.

Solso concluded his chapter on visual cognition with an important point for the goal of our proposal. He stated, "The Gestalt laws of perceptual organization were fertile ground in which the aspirations of modern cognitive psychologists could grow" (p. 99). Even though other laws of perceptual organization may be simpler and less subjective, "There is little disagreement that the Gestalt patterns of perceptual organization are major factors in determining how objects are perceived" (p. 99). Solso proposed that the comprehension of complex visual stimuli "begins by distinguishing salient featural components that are then recombined in the mind's eye. The aesthetic experience is greater than the sum of the parts but it begins with parts" (p. 99), and the Gestalt factors organize them into a meaningful structure for us.

Context

Anderson (1985) and Solso (1994) discussed "context" as a top-down cognitive function or as that part of perception that is affected by higher-order cognitive functions. That is, high-order general knowledge that we store in our long-term memory determines the interpretation of low-level perceptual units. Context has two features affecting the interpretation of what we see that can be added to the Gestalt principles: the physical composition of the visual field and the personal history of the viewer (Solso, 1994, p. 101). The physical context has a substantial impact on basic perception. Solso discussed "contrast" as one of the major impacts of context. *Brightness contrast* displays the influence of context on the perceived intensity of an object: Light backgrounds make foregrounds or enclosed objects darker (p. 106). Lightness and darkness are also cues for distance and thus can signify the apparent nearness of an object. Perception is also strongly influenced by contextual knowledge, which includes the inferences and expectations of the viewer. Many experiments have shown that the mind fills in or identifies the meaning of what it sees simply from the context in which the object and viewer are embedded. This holds for words and handwriting, geometric figures, and even larger visual environments.

Attention

"It is likely that visual attention in the human adult is driven by intention, interest, previous knowledge, movement, unconscious motivation, and context" (Solso, 1994, p. 136). Cowan (1995) drew from Gestalt psychologists Kohler and Koffka the following definition: *Attention* is a special attitude of simple unspecific directedness toward an object. This directedness supplies the energy that is required to detect patterns (Anderson, 1985) from the chaos of full perceptual activity. Attention can be directed outward to stimuli or inward to long-term memories (LTM) by the mechanism of awareness. In this context, attention and awareness could be considered a subset or process of short-term activated memory interacting outwardly with the components of perception or inwardly with the components of our stored knowledge. As for our LCD interest in scaffolding the learning process, we know that those things that have had more attention paid to them will encode better in LTM and be easier to retrieve at a later time. Sustaining or engaging attention to gain adequate encoding strength will become an important factor in LCD, and it will be the role of perceptual design elements to carry most of the responsibility for this task.

Peripheral Perception and Scanning

The layout of information determines the ease with which the human visual system can navigate around a display. Control of eye movements is required in scanning all forms of visual information, whether, graphic or text. A major difference between visual and verbal stimuli lies in their spatial frequency. Words of the same font represent a stimulus of high but consistent spatial frequency. A picture represents a more variable stimulus with some areas of higher and lower frequency. Pictures thus have increased identifiability in peripheral vision due to their low spatial frequency—their inconsistencies. Besides simply noting the numerous advantages of graphics, some helpful textual design principles include the following: (a) Displays will be easier to scan if they allow for some discrimination in peripheral vision; (b) The smoother the font, the more readable; (c) It is recommended not to right-justify, as it removes an attention cue; and (d) Spacing between paragraphs must be sufficient to provide perceptual cues of the end of one and the beginning of another thought (Landsdale and Ormerod, 1994).

Anderson (1985): Perception and Information Flow

Anderson (1985) synthesized much of the perception research when he described a model of the flow of information during perception: A stimulus arrives from the environment via sensory processes, which start to organize it through the application of edge detection and the Gestalt principles of proximity, similarity, and continuation, and so on. The result of this process is held in sense memory as a segmented feature description. To this content of memory are applied attention, context, and feature combination strategies in an overall pattern recognition process. The resulting pattern is stored in activated, or working, memory. With a continued focus of attention or awareness, it undergoes top-down pattern identification and begins to be encoded into long-term memory for storage and retrieval at a later date.

Moving back to the question of imagery or the storage of images in memory, Anderson postulated that there is a separate level of representation for images. From pattern recognition and identification processes, there is the formation of a cognitive representation that he termed *perception-based knowledge*. Properties of such an image representation are different from an actual picture because the image representation does the following:

- Records spatial structure
- Records the order of the elements

- Is abstract: in other words, is not an exact copy of what is seen
- Has some operations (such as rotating the image) that are hard to imagine
- Is distorted by user's knowledge
- Consists of parts, which makes hierarchy possible, especially if input is complex

We will look at this form of representation among others in Chapter 5.

Solso (1994): Human Visual Perception

In his book on cognition and the visual arts, Solso (1994) summarized many of the points mentioned above:

> The human sensory system is constantly being stimulated by an enormous amount of information, some of which is important, some trivial, and some worthless. If we processed all stimuli equally, it would not only be a wasteful allocation of energy but would overload a limited processing system. In order to make sense of our world, visual information must be processed rapidly and accurately. Human visual perception utilizes various pattern recognizers, such as those identified by Gestalt psychologists, in the basic organization of features. These features normally appear in context. The combination of features and context is detected by the eye and processed by the mind utilizing the brain's large compendium of knowledge about what the features in the context mean. (pp. 114-116)

From this point forward, in the information-processing flow, our brains move to the classification and representation of the object in long-term memory. These processes (representation and classification) will be discussed in detail in Chapters 5 and 6, respectively.

INFORMATION SCIENCE: INFORMATION DESIGN AND ELEMENTS OF ABSTRACTING

As an organizational reminder to the reader, the first part of this chapter dealt with some elements of the cognitive sciences that deal with perception. This second part deals with closely related topics in the information sciences: namely, visual information and interface design and the principles behind making a good abstract.

Wurman (1989, 1997): Information Design for Understanding and the Management of Complexity

Information design, in terms of the work of Wurman's *Information Architects* (1997), seeks to represent especially complex or especially large amounts of information in ways that can be easily understood by interested individuals. Wurman stated in *Information Anxiety* (1989) that "While numerous fields are involved with the storage and transmission of information virtually none is devoted to translating it into understandable forms for the general public" (p. 55). However, a small cadre of designers are using the power of graphic design to perform this trick of developing understanding out of the seeming chaos of data. It is important to note that this attention to understandability is their specific intention and not a by-product of some more common aesthetic notion. It is this intentional focus on managing complexity toward understanding that aligns the work of information architects with the goals of LCD. Let me extract a few excellent design points from the "information architects" that will give us our first taste of what could be done with content (with the actual information provided by a design), not just its pure perceptual qualities such as the use of color or contrast.

Wurman (1989, 1997) described in some detail the lessons that he has learned over the years about the five major ways in which information can be organized visually (and textually) to support real understanding. He used the mnemonic LATCH as shorthand for these five organization methods. But before I list them, I think it would be useful to put them in the context of how Wurman characterized understanding itself, this being his organizational goal. Perhaps a singular train of thought, seen throughout his work from *Information Anxiety* (1989) to *Information Architects* (1997), can be concisely summarized in his statement that; "learning means making connections," or finding relationships. One understands something new only in relation to something one already understands; thus, understanding is a process of comparison. His search, then, was to find ways by which our ability to compare and connect could be augmented. This is what is done through the process of using LATCH in information design. *LATCH* refers to

1. Organizing information according to *location,* as in portraying the distribution of resources, or of corporate offices, around the world. The U.S. Army recently organized its entire training scheme around two very basic location questions: "Where is the enemy?" and "Where are those

that report to me?" All training should help its soldiers answer at least one of those two questions.

2. Organizing information according to *alphabetical order*. This is good for organizing large data sets like dictionaries, encyclopedias, and telephone books.

3. Organizing according to *time*. This applies best to "events that happen over a fixed duration, such as conventions" (p. 325).

4. Organizing information according to *category*. This is best used in dealing with objects, such as books in a library or models of cars, objects that have a variety of types. Also "this mode lends itself well to organizing items of similar importance" (p. 325). The other useful role of chunking is that you are dividing a complex subject into perceivable and thus understandable parts.

5. Organizing information according to *hierarchy* (or *continuum*). This applies to situations where there is a need to show differences in value: size, weight, importance, or order of command (Norman, 1989).

Tufte (1990, 1997): Visuals That Explain

In this section, we will continue with guidelines and insights from the world of information design as conceived by the prolific and respected Edward Tufte. For Tufte, information design seeks to convey ideas about things that are not materially in our presence. This is achieved by evoking (in graphical form) an appropriate mental representation of the concepts and ideas. Effective design represents objects or concepts by providing only essential elements that are most characteristic of that object or concept. For example, street signs that depict people do not show one specific person (such as a president or celebrity) but provide commonalities, such as two arms, two legs, a torso, and a head, which represent the concept of "person" or "human being." Presenting only essential elements (known as *abstraction*) provides a general representation of a class of similar objects by removing detail that might identify it with a particular subclass.

Visual information and design can induce learning by presenting more than just data. Information is cognitively usable when presented as relationships, process, form, and functionality. In this way, information is not disjointed but appears as a unified whole, spanning time and space, depicting cause-and-effect, and even visualizing abstract ideas. Information design can give a visual picture to ideas and concepts; therefore, it must visually compare and distinguish, group similar information into hierarchies, order information, and show the most substantive pieces of information within a complex structure.

Visualizing information can emphasize complex information that is concrete and stable, as well as dynamic and abstract. Information presented in this manner allows users to grasp complex concepts and to more fully understand, and thus to reason about, the concepts being presented (see Chapter 7 for further discussion of the power of graphical visualization schemes).

Visual information enhances our ability to make decisions in that it can clarify concepts; help depict cause-and-effect relationships; inspect and evaluate alternative explanations of concepts, ideas, or situations; and provide clear comparison of important information. "Clear and precise seeing becomes as one with clear and precise thinking" (Tufte, 1997, p. 53). The visual design of information must be accurate; it must "tell the truth." Comparing information that is visually depicted in different modes could be misleading and bring users to faulty conclusions. The logic of the display design must reflect the logic of the decision-making process that the information engages (Tufte, 1997).

Good information design attacks complexity in a number of ways:

- It portrays "density" by identifying different information elements and visually sharing how they relate to one another.

- It displays complex information in a more unified fashion, providing a general overview of information that may change over time and space or that is dynamic in nature. When similar information elements can be visualized and compared, abstract information becomes more tangible.

- It portrays dimensionality within information that may not easily correlate with the three dimensions familiar to the human mind. Good information design provides order, emphasizing those elements or dimensions that provide meaning or make a difference within the overall design while deemphasizing other elements that could create more clutter or visual noise.

- It provides beauty by using color, strategic placement of information elements, and balance to present complex information or concepts in a meaningful manner. Such design emphasizes a single unified whole whose parts function together synergistically.

Thus, reducing complexity in information design is achieved by using principles such as coherence, by layering and separating data, by "multiplying" images, by using color, and by visually representing space and time.

A coherent interface uses multiple design elements working together to form a larger, single cohesive system that is simple, elegant, and beautiful. Coherence attacks visual clutter by providing consistency in design, such as using color, font, size, and shape repetitiously and sparingly. Coherence can provide clarity in information design in that it provides "an understanding of complexity, revealed with an economy of means" (Tufte, 1990, p. 51). Using consistent design elements allows users to become familiar with the presentation and does not add the need to commit small details to memory (Tufte, 1997). For example, within a Web site, collections of similar information can be color coded to identify the broader topic to which specific information belongs. When this is done, users are given immediate cues about the nature of this information, alleviating the need for the user to commit such details to memory.

Layering and separating data reduces complexity and creates learning by placing emphasis on distinctions that make a difference. Layering and separating can group numerous information elements while filtering out non-pertinent information and emphasizing and giving more visual weight to important information. Certain elements are enhanced by using color, increasing size, using boldness, and accenting information or making it more prominent within the visual design. This process also conveys a way of grouping information in a hierarchy and thus ordering the importance of information elements.

Comparison is used to multiply the same image in different stages of context, such as space and time. Comparison allows a visual recording of dynamic information. An example would be a chart of different phases of the moon in which you view a representation of the moon every 24 hours. It becomes apparent that the moon slowly goes from full moon, to half moon, to almost no moon, then slowly back to full moon. In one picture, one is able to see how the moon looks over a 28-day time period. Multiplying images is a powerful tool that allows users to more fully understand complex, dynamic information without reducing it or losing valuable meaning.

Color and contour express relationships by segmenting, joining, or enhancing data elements. Color cognitively attracts attention to data elements without providing excessive clutter or visual "noise." Color invokes harmony among elements. Presenting information as a unified picture or concept reduces the cognitive time needed to comprehend the idea, thereby displaying information while minimizing attention to the design vehicle.

Abstract information is portrayed in information design using pattern recognition. Finding a "narrative" of space and time, or pattern and form, amidst commotion simplifies the essential elements and represents them visually. An example of this is a visual recording, on pen and paper, of different dance steps of a ballet. The focus is on emphasizing the essence of the abstract information by using simplicity, not on adhering to a strict interpretation of visual reality.

Two ideas that stand out in Tufte's work are abstraction and narrative. Both of these techniques go to the heart of managing complexity, taking away all that is not essential while keeping a narrative coherence to the whole. Tufte's work has ranged from what he called "pictures of numbers" to "pictures of nouns" to "pictures of verbs," all using the organization strategies listed by Wurman (1989) above and all aimed at managing cognitive complexity on many fronts. The next authors will give us yet another perspective on the elements of visual design and how they can be used to manage complexity and help deliver user understanding.

Mullet and Sano (1995): Visual Design for Communication

Mullet and Sano's *Designing Visual Interfaces* (1995) is impressive on two levels. First, it presents their design principles from a deep understanding of the cognitive issues involved in perception, categorization, and representation. Second, the organization of the book itself is an example of learner-centered design. Their book is an excellent example of taking very complex principles and organizing them in such a manner as to make their comprehension seem effortless and intuitive.

The book is divided into sets of principles and techniques that guide best practices in design. The following is a list of those principles that are especially relevant to managing cognitive complexity:

- Elegance—comes from a Latin root that means "to choose, elect, or select carefully." Elegance in design means thoughtful selection of the elements to be emphasized in the visual field for maximum cognitive saliency. "Elegance in design is seen in the immediately obvious success of a novel approach that solves a problem completely yet in a highly economical way" (p. 17). And in direct application to my approach to LCD, the authors related this elegance in design to simplicity:

    > In fact, the sheer simplicity of an elegant solution is often its most startling and delightful aspect. Elegant solutions reveal an intimate understanding of the problem and an ability to ensure that its essence is grasped by the consumer as well. (p. 17)

    This design principle is like the Strunk and White (1979) (minimalist writing guidelines) version of visual communication: Get to the point, and leave out all that is not essential.

- Simplicity—stresses the minimization of component parts and the simplification of the relationships between those parts. To achieve simplicity and elegance, the authors suggested the use of three key principles: unity, refinement, and fitness. *Unity* means that all the individual components work together toward a common purpose. *Refinement* (or parsimony) is the process by which anything that is not essential to the communication task is removed. This is accomplished iteratively through progressive abstraction of the essence of the elements. *Fitness* (or utility) ensures that after unity and refinement have been accomplished, the design still performs its essential function or communicative duty. Typical examples of these three principles at work can be found in the simple, but functional, design of Shaker furniture. Practical techniques for reducing complexity include (a) reducing a design to its essence or finding the essential elements and then finding the essential form of those elements, (b) regularizing the elements of the design or using repeating or standard patterns, and (c) combining elements such that a single element plays multiple roles.

Organization is another set of principles emphasized by the authors and is similar to Wurman's notions listed above. The following is a list of the elements of organization in design:

- *Grouping* adds structure. By grouping similar elements together, the designer helps the user deal with a complex information display by reducing it to a manageable number of units. Higher-level structures, columns, paragraphs, and sections orient the user and help him or her to establish a plan for moving his or her attention to some interesting portion of the display for a more detailed reading (p. 94).

- *Hierarchy* adds order. When the elements or groups of a display vie for attention, hierarchy allows for the direction of attention to facilitate the intended communication. *Hierarchy* in this case means attracting the attention of the user through dominance of size or color or both.

- *Relationship* supports the design elements of grouping and hierarchy. "Relations between elements can be based on any of the visual variables, but the dominance of position, size, and value provide the most effective cues" (p. 99). Of these, position is the most powerful: "The eye is very sensitive to alignment, as witnessed by the Gestalt phenomena of 'good continuation'" (p. 99).

In summary, we can link all these elements together. If we have used the principles of elegance and refined each element of the visual display to its essence while maintaining a systemic unity among them, we are ready to chunk the elements according to function and establish a visual hierarchy of importance using position, size, and so on. Finally, when "this hierarchy is clear, the display itself can be structured to reflect the relationships between the elements while maintaining a pleasing balance" (p. 98). Beauty and understandability go hand in hand.

Cremmins (1982): Creating Abstracts

Here we move away from graphical information design to a unique form of textual design. I have included it in this chapter on perception because of the uncanny commonality between the cognitive process and goals of creating visual designs and those of creating the perfect abstract, not to mention the explicit missions of both to attack complexity and provide understanding. An abstract is defined by the American National Standards Institute as "an abbreviated, accurate representation of the contents of a document, preferably prepared by its author for publication with it" (Cremmins, 1982, p. 3). In general, abstracts contain up to four sequential information elements that describe or extract information from the basic document. These elements state the "purpose, methodology, results, and conclusions presented in the original document" (p. 5).

Abstracts help simplify the reader's reaction to information. They help readers decide if the material "contains information that will satisfy their needs" (p. 4) and if they should consult the full text of the material.

There are four stages to the cognitive act of abstracting:

1. Focusing on the basic features of the materials

2. Identifying relevant information

3. Extracting, organizing, and reducing the relevant information into a coherent unit

4. Refining the completed abstract through editing (Cremmins, 1982)

Good abstracting requires good reading, thinking, writing, and editing skills. Analytical reading for abstracting involves actively reading for information content and passively reading for understanding. (Conversely, Cremmins stated that reading actively for understanding and passively for information content is more appropriate for more complex research and writing activities.)

In the first or retrieval reading stage of abstracting, the abstractor reads quickly through the text to find sections containing relevant information. In the second or creative reading stage, the abstractor rereads the material to select, extract, organize, and write the most relevant information for the abstract. During the final or critical reading stage, the abstractor reads the written abstract analytically to edit for unity and conciseness and to ensure that the abstract complies with any stylistic rules and conventions (Cremmins, 1982, p. 22). It is here that we clearly find resonance between the production of abstracts and Mullet and Sano's (1995) principle of elegance in design, with its subtasks of finding a balance between unity and refinement while maintaining a fitness for its intended purpose.

The thinking skills necessary for abstracting are similar to those used in problem solving. Cremmins cited M.C. Beardsley's assertion that such thinking "takes imagination, sensitivity, persistence, concentration, and the ability to obtain and connect much relevant information. But without some skill in logic, the task is hopeless" (p. 78).

The process of writing and editing primarily involves reducing the information for the reader. Writing abstracts should be an "all-out effort in information reductionism or condensation, regardless of the style, content, or form required for the abstract" (p. 9). Paraphrasing style writer William Strunk, Cremmins offered the following advice: "Omit needless paragraphs, sentences, and words and phrases within sentences" (p. 9).

From this description of the abstract process, we can see the resonance with the approach and intention of Wurman, Tufte, and Mullet and Sano. The singular purpose of all these authors is to take the complex, whether this complexity is due to massive amounts of data or to the intellectually challenging nature of the subject, or to the attempt to communicate and coach through a two-dimensional medium, and to transform it into something elegant, understandable, and enjoyable.

SUMMARY

The following perception-based design principles facilitate the management of complexity through the reduction of neural load during a learner's interaction with an information design:

- Consistency—the extent to which something lacks variation

- Coherence—the extent to which something presents a complete picture

- Affordance—the extent to which the perceived properties of something are consistent with its actual properties

- Essence—the basic style and content element, whether in simplicity, refinement, or abstracting

- Elegance—simplicity; unity, refinement, and fitness

- Visualization

- Color and Position—its proper use for grouping and attention

- Narrative—maintaining coherence

INTERACTIVE-INFORMATION-FIELD DESIGN: EXAMPLES AND LESSONS

This section discusses systems that are powerful organizers but have struggled for acceptance due to difficult learning curves, initial complexity, or simply being ahead of their time. Along with some aspects of the systems discussed above, systems that allow for richness of functionality, cross-linking organization, and variety and dynamic growth are often perceived as too complex for the average user or too expensive in the learning curve and have given way to the traditional systems that better fit the status quo. Only when simpler learning curves have been designed into the product, as in the case of a Macintosh desktop graphical user interface (GUI) or Windows 95 or a Mosaic interface for the Internet, has the complexity of the organization behind the interface been overridden and the tool been widely accepted. The lesson is that a knowledge organization tool may be designed with many positive factors, including good cognitive rules, but the cognitive complexity of the interface may keep the tool from being accepted unless it is for a specialized audience of experts or unless people come to see the tool's overriding intrinsic value. LCD contends that any powerful yet awkward system, redesigned with learner-centered design principles, can reduce its learning curves to such an extent that they can be successfully placed in the hands of wider and wider audiences. There is a secondary lesson here also. Systems that provide a recognized valuable return will find acceptance despite any interface difficulties. Content and understandability become more important to these users than learnability and usability.

The Bloomberg Business Machine

The success of this specialized information system has been phenomenal. For its careful and simplifying design of complex and overwhelming daily financial content, users have held it in high esteem, and Bloomberg was able to build a communications empire based on its acceptance.

In 1982, Michael Bloomberg formed a company to develop a financial markets terminal that would provide bankers and Wall Street money managers with data graphs, charts, numbers, and other up-to-the-moment information. There are now more than 75,000 Bloomberg terminals in financial offices around the world, generating about $1 billion in annual revenue. Bloomberg also started a global news wire, Bloomberg News, carried by hundreds of newspaper; the 24-hour Bloomberg News Radio; Bloomberg Information TV; and magazines, a Web site, and other products. Bloomberg has become the number one financial quotation service, according to a recent Business Wire survey, of 500 financial services/banking executives. Dow Jones, Reuters, and

Business Wire were cited as the top three desktop delivery/newswire services (A. Kirkpatrick, personal communication, 1997).

Informal user surveys of the Bloomberg terminals tell us that acceptance is 99% about content. The system has a compelling breadth of content but is also allegedly tougher to learn than Dow Jones or Reuters. The interface is actually cumbersome. There is no ease of entry. There are unusual commands. You don't use the enter key, for instance. But once you become an expert, these deficiencies are overlooked. Bloomberg's data, financial statistics, are more in-depth, more historical. The system has everything: In addition to financial data on companies, currencies, bonds, stocks, and so on, it also has airline schedules, a dictionary, and an Old English dictionary. Eventually, if there is a market reversal and people start to cut back on services, I think they're going to say, "Why do I need these other systems?" Bloomberg has created a brand. Now when I think of data, I wonder, "How will I get that out of Bloomberg?" Despite the difficulty of the interface, it has some nice features also. It is very easy—one step—to get all the news on one single topic, such as gold or the tobacco companies. It also includes e-mail so the subscribers to the service can e-mail each other. The message here is that a very rewarding content can survive a cumbersome interface (A. Kirkpatrick, personal communication, 1997).

The Network Computer Interface

Halfhill (1997) introduced the latest significant design change since 1984 in his article "Good-Bye, GUI, Hello NUI." An *NUI* is a network user interface. NUIs offer the following:

- A consistent browser like interface for navigating local and remote file systems

- The ability to display Java programs and other dynamic Web content without a Web browser

- Replacement of the manipulation of direct representations of resources with the use of hyperlinks to navigate and bring up remote resources

- The ability to automatically update dynamic content using push and pull webcasting technologies

- A shifting in complexity away from the client end and toward professionally managed servers

- The building of interfaces that are customized for the actor as individual information user

Part of the NUI impact has been a rethinking of GUIS: "Software engineers are reconsidering old assumptions and applying new knowledge. Some NUIS discard features that cause trouble for casual users, such as double clicking, overlapping windows, hierarchical menus, and hieroglyphic button bars" (Halfhill, 1997, p. 64).

NUIS are adapted to the browser-based activity and power of the Web as a open-hyperdoc system. The effects of this new environment are not yet fully developed, but the design principles we have covered above will still apply because they are based on cognitive principles that have not changed.

PERCEPTION AND INFORMATION DESIGN: MANAGING COMPLEXITY

The complexity scales from Chapter 3 most directly affected by the elements of perception and information design are the metasocial forces, information overload, and design word-pair scales.

Cognitive Complexity Word-Pair Scales

Table 4.2 lists the origins and elements of cognitive complexity due to metasocial forces, information overload, and design.

Table 4.2.   Origins and Elements of Complexity Due to Metasocial Forces, Information Overload, and Design

Origin	Elements of Complexity						
	Novelty						Confirmation
	7	6	5	4	3	2	1
	Dynamic						Stable
	7	6	5	4	3	2	1
Metasocial Forces and Information Overload	Variety						Redundancy
	7	6	5	4	3	2	1
	Disorder						Order
	7	6	5	4	3	2	1
	Noise						Signal
	7	6	5	4	3	2	1

Table 4.2. Origins and Elements of Complexity Due to Metasocial Forces, Information Overload, and Design *(Continued)*

Origin	Elements of Complexity						
	Approximate						Precise
	7	6	5	4	3	2	1
	Hidden						Apparent
	7	6	5	4	3	2	1
	Nonstandardized					Standardized	
Design	7	6	5	4	3	2	1
	Illogical						Logical
	7	6	5	4	3	2	1
	Obscure						Obvious
	7	6	5	4	3	2	1
	Unbounded					Constrained	
	7	6	5	4	3	2	1

LCD Recommendations

Recommendations for the Design of System Content

Our understanding and use of the principles of perception are most often explicitly oriented toward developing system competency, namely learnability and usability (see following text). But if understanding is a matter of making associations and connections, especially through comparison, then elements of good interface design can be applied to the design of content as well. I believe that the following are good principles to use with content development:

- Use visuals to portray complex dynamic data.
- Use the Wurman LATCH mnemonic to organize information.
- Use a sense of narrative to maintain coherency.
- Use natural dialogue.
- Break content into understandable parts.
- Use terms and language familiar to the expected users.
- Provide a context for the concepts being discussed.
- Reduce content to that which is essential.

- Progressively refine text to the most relevant.
- Present content in groups or classes.
- Ensure unity of content and avoid fragmentation.
- Reveal patterns in the content.

Recommendations for the Design of System Use

This chapter's topics and principles have been available for the design of GUIS and other examples of information-fields for over two decades. It is my contention that when they have been applied (not applying these principles is the main stumbling block) these best practices naturally work well for complexity management and will continue to be a core of best practices for LCD. When I look at the effect of perception-based visual design, my recommendations emphasize those principles that most directly attack the design complexity scales.

On the perceptual level, we have two concerns: the components or elements of the interface and the whole or Gestaltlike organizing nature of our perceiving processes. As was quoted above, Solso (1994) proposed that the comprehension of complex visual stimuli "begins by distinguishing salient featural components that are then recombined in the mind's eye. The aesthetic experience is greater than the sum of the parts but it begins with parts" (p. 99), and the Gestalt factors organize them into a meaningful structure for us.

Design principles of perception that guide us in the search for simplicity are a matter of supporting the following perceptual organization cues as applied to parts and wholes:

- Parts—of the interface of the information-field

  - Similarity, proximity
  - Refinement and reduction, fitness
  - Relationship
  - Scale
  - Consistency

- Whole—interface of the information-field as a system

  - Pattern recognition
  - Structure—canonical grid
  - Continuation, closure, *Pragnanz*
  - Unity
  - Grouping or classification
  - Hierarchy of groups
  - Coherency—system acts as an integrated whole

CONCLUSION

The topics of this chapter and the next really act as a matched pair, because the interaction of a consumer, a student, or a worker, with an interface of any sort is guided at its most basic levels by the laws of both perception and model building (Chapter 5). Thus, the concepts and precepts of the first two chapters of Part II, the first two levels of our cognitive hierarchy, are very intertwined, and there should be much overlap in the design guidelines they recommend. What is unique and prescient in this chapter is our initial look at an approach to "designing for understanding" by the practitioners of information design (i.e., by Tufte and Wurman); an approach that puts a tremendous emphasis on communicating the message in the medium. Thus, we have early on gone beyond the surface and organizational elements of "designing for perception" alone and gone straight to the heart of designing for meaning. This is key to LCD because one of its main focuses is on the understandability of content, and Wurman and Tufte are masters of designing content for maximum understanding. We will revisit their content design principles throughout the remaining chapters.

Now let us move on to the next level of cognitive hierarchy and the next level of design considerations concerned with managing the complexity of the human-to-information-field interaction. In doing just that, Chapter 5 deals with representing knowledge and the responsibility of designers to facilitate the creation of efficient and effective mental models in the minds of those that use their products.

5

Learner as Model Builder

To my mind the major accomplishment of cognitive science has been the clear demonstration of the validity of positing a level of mental representation: a set of constructs that can be invoked for the explanation of cognitive phenomenon, ranging from visual perception to story comprehension.

—Howard Gardner

ABOUT THIS CHAPTER

The LCD focus of this chapter is on the nature of mental models for learners. This chapter includes discussions and examples from

- Cognitive science on problem solving and representation
- Information science on cognitive systems engineering and hypertext

The resulting design principles are extracted and listed at the end of the chapter.

INTRODUCTION

In Chapter 9, we will discuss explicit scaffolding or support strategies for "learners as students," emphasizing design elements that facilitate the construction of mental models that are concerned with understanding content. But before we do that, in this chapter, we are going to introduce the idea of mental models through the more general concept of *knowledge representation*. Our goal is to arrive at some general LCD guidelines for learnability, usability, and understandability at a level above those suggested by the laws of perception. In doing so, we will incorporate early work done on representation and human problem solving and later work done by Norman (1986) and others that came to be known as *user-centered design* (UCD). This is an important consideration early in our discussion because LCD is in many ways an extension of the principles of UCD. Following the organization of Chapter 4, we will move through our cognitive and information science topics, representation and hypertext, and then finish with a critique of some actual systems and our LCD recommendations.

THE ORGANIZATION OF RESEARCH INTO REPRESENTATION

Representation is the general concept used to describe a symbolic level of knowledge organization and information processing within memory. What we know is stored internally in the form of various kinds of knowledge formats or representations. In this introduction to representation, we will move down a hierarchical tree of discussion points to those portions of research into this concept that will be most useful to us in discovering design principles.

Cognitive scientists tend to agree that there is a need to describe the cognitive functions of planning, classification, language, and problem solving at a level that is above the very concrete view of how the nervous system works and yet below broadly abstract cultural influences. For this in-between "individual-cognitive" level of representation, they posit either of the following:

- One form of representation for all mental objects, consisting of statements and rules

- At least two forms or representation: one type for textual representation and a second type for holding images

Several models and conceptual frameworks have been constructed in an effort to characterize this cognitive representational level—scripts, schemas, symbols, frames, images, and mental models—and to describe the operations that are carried out upon these mental entities: assimilation, accommodation, transformations, conjunctions, deletions, and reversals. For my purpose, I use the term *mental model* to mean any general form of textual or image representation.

From one research perspective, there are two states of these representations:

1. Those involved in the unconscious processing of perceptions into symbolic representations of physical or sensory input

2. Those involved in the problem solving and classification that individuals carry out with some degree of explicitness and awareness (Gardner, 1985)

LCD is concerned with both, but in emphasizing learning we will stress the latter. Delving further, within this research we find the study of either of the following:

- The rationale for representations: that is, how frames, scripts, schemas, or mental models answer many questions about the process of storage and retrieval in memory and their structure in different domains

- Research on how these structures are constructed during the learning process

Again, LCD concentrates upon the latter, defining learning as the active and explicit construction of stable, long-term mental models of topics or procedures that may or may not involve special representations of images.

In overview, Johnson-Laird (1990) described the five subtopics of research into representation:

1. *Perception (or visual representation).* Among others, Marr's theory of visual representation depends on the construction of a series of symbolic representations that culminate in a three-dimensional model of the spatial relations among the objects involved. This model makes explicit the location of objects to our conscious processes of judgment and thereby enables us to navigate our way through the world, avoiding obstacles and hazards. Of course, what we perceive is not actuality but an interpretation that depends on the constraints of our sensory system in conjunction with what we know of the world.

2. *Representation of speech.* In representational theory, abstract models of speech are produced, as opposed to remembering the explicit words of what was said. This has been corroborated over and over again by Schank, Bransford, and others. There is also abundant evidence that the coherence of a conversation or text passage depends on how easy it is to construct a single mental model of it. "Passages calling for a single model of spatial layout are easier to remember than indeterminate descriptions that may be consistent with more than one layout" (Johnson-Laird, 1990, p. 472).

3. *Representation of reasoning processes.* There are three theories of reasoning: (a) Reasoning depends on general rules for drawing conclusions, such as the rules of logic, which work regardless of content or the specific situation; (b) Reasoning depends on content-specific rules, which explains why context sometimes makes a difference in the conclusions people draw; and (c) Reasoning is carried out by manipulating mental models. The mental model theory of reasoning is based on the belief that in order to reason correctly, people first need to understand the premises of the situation they are reasoning about: In other words, they need to create a mental model of the reasoning context. Next, they construct a model of an hypothesis that explains the situation and test it out by searching for other models that can be used as counterexamples. In fitting with the concerns of LCD, Johnson-Laird discussed the difficulty people have in dealing with the cognitive load imposed when more than one model fits an explanation. This idea of load is of interest to us because it exemplifies the complexity that we are trying to manage. For example, if we are presenting an interface to a user and the design of that interface lacks coherence such that the user might develop two or more models of how to interact with its elements, he or she will be forced to test out which of these models contains the correct hypothesis. This testing of multiple interpretations and multiple hypotheses increases the cognitive load on the user and severely reduces the efficiency of the user's learning process (Norman, 1988).

4. *Representation of knowledge.* There has been a significant amount of work done in the cognitive sciences on mental models as the content of mental representations. Researchers have looked at the learning of medical diagnosis techniques, physics, electrical circuits, and so on and have described the process of learning as the development of a mental model of the knowledge that it entails. Johnson-Laird (1990) pointed out that these models appear to be the same as regular mental representations. The key questions for researchers are (a) what is the process by which models are constructed and manipulated and (b) whether there is any advantage to providing people with explicit models of what they are trying to learn (Posner, 1990). I believe there is an advantage, but these are the key questions for LCD as well.

5. *Expertise.* Developing mental models of knowledge and learning has been most often studied in the context of work on expertise (see Chapter 8). In the study of intellectual development, there has been a shift away from the traditional Piagetian emphasis on change in structure and process to change in the content of knowledge. We can see that as one becomes more competent in a domain, one develops a richer model of the subject. (Other more detailed theories are being developed

but are still in their infancy at this time.) An important difference between the way a novice and an expert reason is found in the structure of their mental models. Novices' mental models represent objects and processes that they see in the real world, whereas experts construct models that are more abstract (see Chapter 8 for further distinctions).

Our goal in this context is to discover how the principles of efficient and effective mental model "construction" can be made into explicit LCD guidelines. Early on, cognitive and information scientists studied applications, such as word processors, and naturally focused their attention on learnability and usability issues, with little attention to scaffolding understanding of content (given that these were very knowledge-lean products where content could be ignored). The key shift in the products of our information-fields (in modern appliances from VCRS to palm pilots, information systems like the Internet, and high-tech information-dependent workspaces) is that their content—the information they are trying to communicate or help organize—is rapidly becoming their most salient feature. As this trend continues, in addition to the traditional usability issues, content-centered, learner-centered design will grow in importance, as will our increased dependence on understanding the nature of mental models and representation.

Thus, we are interested in two questions: (a) How can mental models be efficiently constructed and manipulated in the learning process through the elements of LCD, and (b) what instructional form should the system content take (examples, definitions, concepts, analogies)? For example, if I am working in a hypertext system, how can the information architecture or framework be presented to me so that I most efficiently learn how to navigate the system and find relevant material? Also, once I find material on a topic, I want to make certain that its instructional format consists of the elements I need to construct a useful and thus understanding-based model of the topic. We will explore these questions below and again in Chapter 9, "Learner as Student." Given this background, we now want to look at some actual cognitive science research into models and their precursor research topic, problem solving.

Cognitive Science: Models and Authors

Cognitive Psychology: Information-Processing Approach

In the information-processing approach (IPA), the conceptual organization of the thinking process can be divided into three major functional arenas: knowledge acquisition, knowledge representation/organization, and knowledge retrieval.

Knowledge acquisition has been studied as perception and categorization; knowledge representation/organization as memory and mental models; and knowledge retrieval as heuristics, induction, problem solving, and symbol manipulation.

According to the IPA, there is a distinction between learning and problem solving. The IPA is mostly concerned with "knowledge-lean problem solving" (Posner, 1990), which is a purposeful oversimplification of the problem-solving process where learning is considered somewhat of a side issue. However, the IPA also supports the development of problem solving with learning. The following discussion is useful in its clarification of terms and for giving us an understanding of the origin, interest, and power of the "mind as a computer" model developed by Newell and Simon (1972). We will see reverberations of this approach in much of the other research discussed in this and later chapters. Chapter 9 describes schema- or mental-model-driven problem solving in more detail.

In the IPA, the internal representation process of the problem solver generates three elements that combine to become the problem space. They are (a) the initial problem state, (b) operators that can change that state, and (c) a test that can determine if the new state is the solution to the initial problem.

Given this initial state of the problem solver, there is no telling how many, in what order, or which of the operators available is going to lead to the solution. So a search process for the successful operators ensues. This is not a random process but in human problem solving seems to follow heuristics or guiding strategies for selecting and testing operators. These guides exist in two general collaborating processes called the *backup strategy* and the *proceed strategy*. The most common heuristics used are called forward chaining, backward chaining, and difference reduction. Forward chaining starts with the initial state and moves toward the goal. Backward chaining starts with the goal in mind and moves backwards toward the initial state. Heuristics such as these are innate scaffolding devices and serve to narrow the search for the correct operators or problem transformers.

But what about learning in the IPA sense? How do the operators and heuristics form more permanent and efficient ways of solving a problem over time (Posner, 1990)? After all, we are interested in principles of "learner"-centered design.

Learning in the IPA sense occurs in the following ways: compounding and tuning. *Compounding* means formally combining a set of operators that function well together in certain goal situations and making that combination available for future use on similar problems. *Tuning* is the refinement of the heuristics used in the selection of the appropriate operators. With practice, one can see whether a specific heuristic is yielding the best solutions or whether it needs to be modified. Extensions of compounding and tuning occur in the theory of learning based on the use of "productions." A production is a linked set of heuristics, preconditions, and appropriate operators (other processes are associated with productions, including chunking, proceduralization, strengthening, and rule induction, but they are beyond the scope of our mission here.)

Using the IPA model to study cognitive function, psychologists have adopted three fundamental propositions that make up the standard information-processing paradigm (Gardner, 1985; Posner, 1990):

1. Thinking is a serial or sequential process, with serial lines of thought running in parallel when needed.

2. Information flows (input-process-output-feedback).

3. Operators or objects are the basic units of thought or thinking activity.

Under the IPA rubric, problem solving consists of representation and heuristic search processes as follows:

1. The problem space which consists of an internal representation of (a) the initial givens or problem, which may or may not be well defined; (b) the final goal or solution state, which also may or may not be well defined; (c) operators or processes for moving from one state to the next; and (d) subgoals, representing intermediary states between the initial problem and the final solution.

2. The search for, or the application of, techniques (heuristics) for creating subgoals and generally moving along solution paths until the goal state is met (Newell & Simon, 1972). Goals become the clarifying force in much of this process (as in most learning).

In summary, IPA contributions to problem solving and learning are as follows:

- Problem solving is primarily a search of the internal problem space.

- Problem solving is a function of the relationship of the problem solver and the problem's environmental context.

- Pattern recognition reduces the effort of processing facts individually and speeds up understanding or the generalizability of insight.

- People use heuristics, or general templates, in solving problems as a means of selecting relevant information from the totality of information available. Heuristics are often faster than serial algorithms in solving problems. See Chapter 8 for more on heuristics.

- Problem solving involves the creation of a mental model.

Table 5.1 summarizes several other learning theories and their problem-solving modalities. Meaning theory, especially, gives us a few more candidates for LCD guidelines in the design of understandable content. (See Chapter 9 for more details on the contributions of meaning theory.)

Table 5.1.   Learning Theory and Problem-Solving Modes

Learning Theory	Problem-Solving Mode
Associationist	Trial and error (nondirected thinking)
Connectionist	Activation of weighted chains beyond trial and error
Gestalt	Reorganization (of existing information)
Meaning theory	Assimilation (compare to known)
	Relate to user's experience
	Use terms familiar to user
	Make concrete
	Use imagery
	Discovery through activity
	Priming prior to new material
Cognitive theory (neo-connectionist)	Development of productions and mental models
	Development of weighted associations in a neural net

Later in this chapter, we will see the IPA ideas absorbed into the theories of Norman and other cognitive engineers in their search for user-centered design principles based on a solid cognitive foundation. Now let us take a look at further research into representation.

Anderson (1985)

Anderson's (1985) text on cognitive psychology outlined a hierarchy of representation that categorizes the types of representations possible while organizing them in a convenient manner for our own understanding. The following is an outline of his presentation, working from the bottom of the hierarchy on up.

Representation as the Encoding of Information

- Neural Representation—Organization of information at the level of nerve cells, which comes into play with neural networks

- Sense Memory Representation—Gestalt organization of attention and perception patterns in visual and auditory sense memory; includes pattern recognition

- Perception-Based Representation—Elements of sense memory are chunked, spatial elements are recorded, and the order of perceptual elements is tracked; such representation allows for the detection of a hierarchy in perception

- Meaning-Based Representation—Record of interpretation of text or image in long-term memory; simple encoding takes the form of propositions and links or semantic nets; concepts are encoded as schemas or mental models

Mental models are designed as associative matrices. By *matrix,* I mean a tablelike structure that contains attributes and values. Attributes of mental models may be propositions (either meaning based or perception based). These matrices can then be linked via their attributes or their values to other knowledge tables, creating an associative network of interrelated concepts. Ultimately, this associative network becomes cognitive psychology's model of how knowledge is built and stored in memory.

Mental Models and Problem Solving

- Models and their role in problem solving:
  - Valuable as "chunkers"
  - Somewhat inflexible
  - Need to draw on other knowledge structures in unusual situations
  - Need to combine models to form new categories to match new circumstances
  - Stored in LTM as new or modified structures or production systems
  - Creation of mental models is the force behind induction
- Production systems consist of
  - Condition-action/if-then rules
  - Facts to be matched as initiating conditions
  - A method for resolving conflicts between different rules that match the same situation
  - Rules to carry out actions and other elements beyond our LCD mission

We will see the terminology of Anderson's hierarchy, and of production systems, used throughout our remaining chapters.

Legrenzi and Girotto (1996): Mental Models in Reasoning and Decision- Making Processes

This research links the study of mental models with research into reasoning and decision making. It studies the effects of information seeking and other

cognitively intense tasks. Two representational phenomena common to information seeking in our reasoning and decision-making processes are as follows:

1. "The tendency to focus on the initial representation of a situation"
   (p. 195) (see Marshall's [1995] description of example usage in
   instruction in Chapter 9)

2. The difficulty of reasoning and making choices under conditions of
   uncertainty

Legrenzi and Girotto (1996) concluded that for information designers it is
critical to focus on design principles that help build the desired representation
of a module, interface, or information architecture in such a way that users get
it right the first time. Due to our normal focusing phenomena, it will be twice
as hard to shift from a primary representation to a second or third at a later
date. It is also noted that the text of a problem has the power to focus or
defocus the user's attention toward the more accurate representation.
Certainly, it will behoove designers to take care in not creating disjunctive
situations either in presentation or in textual content, where more than one
competing model of an interaction or understanding can be formed. The
results of competing models are an increased uncertainty and complexity for
the user that inevitably leads to an increased tendency to misrepresent.

It is also hopeful that even given disjunctive situations, examples and other
techniques can be used to clarify and rectify confusion and errors in judgment.

Now let us take a look at how the study of mental models has been applied
to information science and through the creation of UCD interfaces and then
extend the discussion to more general subjects of design.

Information Science: Contributions From Cognitive Engineering Models and Authors

This section is a brief and selective overview of some of the major contributions to the research surrounding the cognitive approach to information
system design. It is selective in that it aims at beginning the process of mapping
information-field design to cognitive processes, specifically for the purposes of
managing complexity and increasing the learnability and understandability of
the overall user-object interaction. Following one of the organizational suggestions of Wurman's LATCH mnemonic, this review is done in simple chrono-
logical order. Most of the studies included here concern information system
interface design, but I believe that by looking for basic principles it is relatively
easy to generalize these results to our more general target of information-fields
(information, products, workspaces, and so on).

Moran (1981): User Models, Interfaces, and the Cognitive Approach

Moran (1981) defined the user interface as consisting of those aspects of a system that the user comes in contact with physically, perceptually, and conceptually. To design the user interface of a system is to design the user model or the user's conception of how the system operates. However, it is the dominant opinion among many researchers that the system design often imposes the user model and that the diversity of users and their goals and abilities is ignored.

For LCD, the lesson is that in designing for understandability we must design the interface and content using the learners' conceptions of how material is most easily and efficiently understood. After Soloway et al. (1994), this means designing for the users' goal of comprehension, need for motivation, need for flexibility, and need for gradual system adaptation as their understanding grows over time.

Card et al. (1983): GOMS Model

The GOMS model is an attempt to represent specific human problem solving behavior (experts using an interface of an application) in terms of goals, operators, methods, and selection (GOMS) rules after the Newell and Simon (1972) information processing approach (IPA) above. The elements of the GOMS model are referenced here because they are used in other studies below.

Kieras and Bovair (1984): Mental Models in Operating a Device

In one of the seminal experiments on representation and design, Kieras and Bovair (1984) looked at the effect of a certain type of mental model that they termed a "device model" on learning how to operate an unfamiliar piece of equipment. The device model is an understanding of how the device works in terms of its internal structure and processes. Whether having a device model is beneficial or not has been controversial. We do not seem to need them for operating cars or telephones, but we seem to need them for operating computers or VCRs. The authors experiment reached two conclusions: Having a device model resulted in faster learning and better retention, and having a device model helped users to infer other operating procedures. Their experiment also exposed the critical information required for a user to create a device model. The critical information needed to be (a) concrete as opposed to metaphorical; (b) relevant how-it-works information, not deep or complex; and (c) instructional. Sometimes extra instructional information is not necessary if inferences can be readily made from using the device itself. Also, one has to be careful that the instructional information itself is not misleading.

Kieras and Polson (1985): Cognitive Complexity Theory

Kieras and Polson (1985) assumed that the cognitive complexity of a task determined the difficulty in acquisition, transfer, and retention of the skills necessary to perform that task in a given application. Cognitive complexity is a function of the content, structure, and amount of knowledge required to perform a task using a specific application. The authors proposed that application programs be designed to minimize the cognitive complexity of tasks critical to the running of the program correctly. They also proposed the following three models to describe human-computer interaction:

1. A cognitive model—mental processes needed to perform tasks

2. A conceptual model—information architecture developed by the designer

3. A mental model—personal knowledge structure of the user

Their usage of *cognitive complexity* is really very similar to my use of the term, especially in relation to the design and information overload sources of complexity. However, their approach to measuring complexity is essentially quantitative, whereas my description is purely qualitative.

Borgman (1986): Mental Models and Complex Searches

Borgman (1986) carried out an empirical study, based upon mental model theory, which proposed that people trained to develop a mental model of a system would have an enhanced capability to interact with the system, debug errors, and so on. Her results showed that for simple tasks there was no difference between the mental modeling trained group and the procedurally trained group. However, subjects trained with a model performed better on complex tasks that required extrapolation from the basic operations of the system. Scaffolding or providing explicit models in context may be a significant help in fighting complexity and will become an important LCD guideline for both system use (learnability and usability) and system content (understandability).

Daniels (1986): Cognitive Models to Improve Performance of Information Retrieval Systems

Daniels (1986) evaluated the cognitive viewpoint of Library and Information Science in his *Cognitive Models in Information Retrieval* (1986). He stated,

> In recent years in the field of information retrieval, there has been a growing consensus that the entire human-computer system ought to be viewed as an adaptive cognitive system in order for effective interfaces and whole systems to be designed. (p. 273)

The essence of such a design is based on the development of a "user model" depicting a match between the machine and the user on a cognitive level. Suggestions for developing a model included the following:

1. User models should be individual, not canonical, because it is generally not possible to identify the ideal user.

2. Dynamic and static models of the users are required because the system must take into account the user's changing view of the system and the problem at hand.

3. Implicit user models are required in the information retrieval context because user's are usually in an anomalous state of knowledge: That is, they do not know what they need.

4. A user's plan need not be included in the user model because users do not tend to have a plan of action unless they are experts.

5. It is crucial that the level of detail, or granularity, and the types of knowledge that need to be represented in the user model be discovered and included in the design. Also, the information design should focus on evaluation and resolution of competing inferences.

Daniels concluded that "these suggestions also apply to the information retrieval domain, where a wide range of learning capabilities and sophisticated reasoning mechanisms are required, within the context of a complex, dynamic, mixed-initiative interaction with the user" (p. 301). And he suggested for the future that researchers should attempt to discover just what a user's model should contain. Daniels' discussion and conclusions are very similar to those proposed for LCD by Soloway et al. (1994) in that they have the system focus on the user's need to understand. He also confirmed the user's need for different types of knowledge in order to develop an adequate representation of a topic or procedure. This will be the discussion focus of much of Chapter 9.

Polson (1988): Consistency and Inconsistency

What is the impact of consistency on the learning, transfer, and retention of user skills? Difficulties in the acquisition, transfer, and retention of necessary skills are fundamental limitations to both new and experienced users of complex, modern application programs and workstations (Polson, 1988). The results from three transfer experiments demonstrate that consistent user interfaces mediate positive transfer within an application and across different applications. Inconsistent methods block positive transfer because the user must acquire new rules representing the inconsistent interface presentations. It also took these users considerably more time to develop the variety of representations they needed to deal with the inconsistencies they found. The results of these tests showed the magnitude of the effect of consistency and inconsistency in design. Four-to-one reductions in training times were observed in consistent versus inconsistent situations.

Norman (1988): Cognitive Engineering and Beyond

In *The Psychology of Everyday Things*, Norman (1988) provided principles that go beyond the design of interfaces to the design of everyday objects, thus placing the design discussion in a broader context. This broader context coincides with my design goals because, for LCD, "information systems" metaphorically exist everywhere users find themselves in learning situations— at home, at work, and in school. By reversing Norman's (1988) list of "good" design principles, we can deduce the following elements of potential cognitive complexity:

- Not enough information is supplied about the object for the user to build an adequate mental model of how things work (whether in terms of presentation, documentation, or help screens).

- Tasks required to operate the object require extensive use of memory and/or problem-solving skills.

- Mental aids are lacking.

- There is no visual feedback on the results of an action.

- There is no visual display of what actions are possible.

- There is response incompatibility: Things do not look and act like the actions they intend to carry out. The system's feedback is not matched with the user's expectations.

- Lack of constraints on actions allows the user choices between too many options.

- There is no flexibility in allowing for error.

- There are no standards (Norman, 1988).

These points make up most of the *design* word-pairs in our complexity scale. The fact that Norman believed that these design principles apply beyond the design of information system interfaces goes a long way in supporting the contention that LCD principles are valid across a wide area of design concerns and apply to all potential information-fields that require learning and the processing of information in order to be used to their full capacity.

Farooq and Dominick (1988): Human-Focused Interface Design

The early design of information systems was based on intuition and limited experience and did not lead to good design in terms of either learnability or usability, and certainly not in terms of understandability. Beginning in the mid-1980s there was a strong shift toward user-oriented systems (Borgman, 1986; Norman, 1986). This shift was spurred by the increasingly widespread usage of personal computers and the subsequent demand for more "user-friendly" systems. During this period, the human-computer interaction special interest group brought together researchers in computer science, psychology, human factors, and so on to look at some of the cognitive and design aspects of interfaces that could improve interactivity. Some of this research focused on attempting to understand the human processes involved in comprehending and manipulating a complex system; some looked at evaluating existing design; and some looked at the future of design capabilities. All of it has led to design principles.

In presenting a rationale for the development of formal tools and methods for developing interfaces, Farooq and Dominick (1988) cited the following principles developed early on from user interviews: (a) self-descriptiveness of the system, (b) user control, (c) ease of learning, (d) problem-adequate functionality, (e) correspondence with the user's expectations, (f) flexibility in task handling, (g) tolerance for user error, (h) training and user aids, (i) command languages, (j) consistency of system behavior, and (k) designing for a user's conceptualization of the system.

Chen and Dhar (1991): Cognitive Processes and Information Retrieval Systems Design

Chen and Dhar (1991) applied Ramaprasad's "cognitive process" approach to an analysis of intelligent retrieval in information systems. A typical document-based retrieval system consists of a database of documents, a classification scheme to index the documents, and an on-line system to access the documents. The basic cognitive task for users of such a retrieval system is effective search. The authors created representations of search strategies and tested them out for effectiveness.

In the study, they found that a searcher's knowledge affects his or her formulation of the problem and his or her selection of search strategies in the areas of first methods used, as well as in follow-up refinements. The use of search strategies strongly affected outcome:

- Strong search methods arose in situations where the searcher was stimulated from knowledge about the domain, the classification scheme, and the system. By exploiting regularities in the task environment, such methods produced behavior that was more effective and efficient for the problem at hand. Examples of strong search methods include known-item instantiation, search-option heuristics, and thesaurus-browsing.

- Poor or weak strategies, such as using the trial-and-error search heuristic or screen browsing, corresponded to the natural problem-solving heuristics of means-end and goal-reduction, which require no special task-related knowledge but also produced simpler and less effective searches. It is important for designers to note that these strategies were the ones most often used by searchers.

- Query articulation or refinement resulted from applying search strategies. Searchers went through two phases: (a) the general or broad search, which the authors characterized, after Belkin, as resulting from not really having an identifiable query but only an "anomalous state of knowledge," and (b) refining of the search from this initial state into a formal query, which was an interactive process. The system did not provide interactive refinement help, so the authors concluded that the users were applying strong search strategies at this point. Librarians were particularly adept at the refinement process.

Now that the authors had identified the strong search heuristics that were naturally occurring, they proposed an information retrieval system design that explicitly contained analogues to these search strategies, thus modeling the design after the "cognitive process." They concluded that an information retrieval system would match the cognitive processes best if it had the following components or knowledge sources:

- *On-line thesaurus*—simulating thesaurus-browsing strategy

- *Heuristic-keyword searcher*—simulating the search-option heuristic strategies

- *Task-oriented blackboard architecture*—simulating the known-item instantiater strategy (the blackboard consists of a user model, a task model, a query model, index terms, and citations retrieved)

This is an extremely important study for LCD because it seeks to externalize successful cognitive processes into a design for support of a complex activity. This is going to be one of the major tasks of LCD: to identify cognitive processes, make them explicit, and design them in to facilitate understanding.

Rudnicky (1993): Input Devices Design

Rudnicky (1993) proposed a matrix for matching the input mode to the task. A good interface should supply the input modes that best support the required activities of the user. Most complex applications incorporate several distinct activities. Multiple input modes permit the use of parallel inputs using, for example, voice for mode switching in a graphics application while using a stylus to make changes on an image. Rudnicky proposed that speaking and writing as dual modes of input were both more natural and easier for the machine to learn. Spoken language may be the best mode for queries, whereas commands may be best executed with a pointing device if the number of alternatives is small, as in a small menu selection. Stylus devices appear to be best in situations that require a combination of positional and symbolic input, such as the markup of text or notes. A stylus is not a good device for the entry of extended text. Pointing provides direct access to a location in space that would have to be otherwise selected through spoken or typed coordination.

Crane and Rtischev (1993) also concluded that combining pen and voice technologies will enhance the communication between humans and computers by allowing the strengths of one input method to overcome the weaknesses of the other. The outcome sought from this research is products that will be easier and more natural to use.

The importance of this study for LCD is the idea that "access" is part of any overall design and should not be ignored. This is a matter of ease of use. But another question for LCD could be, What role does the type of access method play in enhancing understandability within an information-field? If access is key to understanding, as Wurman believed, then designing the best method for getting access is also going to be critical.

Marcus (1993): Effective Communication

To enable users to take advantage of advanced applications, product developers need to provide more sophisticated user interfaces. In doing so, they must achieve effective communication of the following user interface elements:

- *Metaphors* are fundamental terms, images, and concepts that are easily recognized, understood, and remembered.

- *Mental models* makeup the appropriate organization and representation of data functions, work tasks, activities, and roles.

- *Model navigation* is the movement among the data functions and activities that provides speedy access to facilitate comprehension (see Chapter 7 on visualization also).

- *Look* is the appearance that efficiently conveys information to the user in an appealing manner.

- *Feel* refers to the interaction techniques that operate efficiently and provide an appealing perceptual experience (Marcus, 1993).

User-centered task-oriented design has become necessary because of (a) the complexity of functions and data, (b) the complexity of user needs, and (c) the unpredictable effects of combinations of products, contents, and form. One way to make products easier to learn and users more productive is to improve the visual communication that takes place at an interface. This includes dealing with the capabilities of the new technologies: agents using macros and expert systems, hypertext, speech input and output, and finally three-dimensional displays, virtual reality, and video.

Madsen: (1994): Metaphor in Design

Metaphor is a powerful form of problem solving and learning. We have seen its effectiveness in the use of the "desktop" metaphor for personal computers for many years. Madsen (1994) reviewed the use of metaphor in the design of a wide range of information systems and gave us a list of guidelines for generating effective interface metaphors: (a) Listen to how users interact with their system, (b) build on already existing metaphors, (c) use predecessor artifacts as metaphors (e.g., using card catalogs as a metaphor allows for the use of previous experience in computerized libraries), (d) note metaphors already implicit in the problem description (e.g., an existing link may stand for a pipe or a path), and (e) look for real-world events exhibiting key aspects of the system.

In evaluating metaphors: (a) Choose metaphors with a rich structure; (b) evaluate the applicability of the structure (i.e., does the structure cover the relevant aspects of the problem?); (c) choose the metaphor suitable to the audience; (d) choose metaphors with well-understood literal meaning—the audience must be familiar with the source of the metaphor, or the transfer of understanding will be inadequate; (e) choose metaphors with a conceptual distance between the source and the metaphorical meaning so that using the metaphor is truly seeing it in another way; (f) have at least one bridging concept that can be strongly related to both the source and the target of the metaphor; and finally, (g) do not necessarily explicitly incorporate the metaphor in the final design, but use it as a thinking tool to help get to the final design.

In developing metaphors: (a) Elaborate the trigger meanings—use them to cover broader elements of the target domain; (b) look for new meanings of the concepts being used—be imaginative and not just literal; (c) restructure the perception of reality; reorder, rename, and regroup existing relations to stimulate the effectiveness of the metaphor for creative thinking; (d) elaborate assumptions, make explicit what the metaphor hides and highlights; (e) identify the unused portion of the metaphor, and seek to consider these properties or features for linkage between the source and target; and (f) generate conflicting accounts based on different metaphors to stimulate critical and creative reflection.

Metaphor is as valuable in understandability as it is in usability. It will be a key part of LCD expressly for its explanatory power (see Chapter 9 for more details on metaphor and content understandability).

Andriole and Adelman (1995): Cognitive Systems Engineering and Organizational Problem Solving

Cognitive systems engineering is equivalent in meaning to the terms *cognitive engineering,* and *cognitive ergonomics.* In looking at the use of cognitive systems engineering for advanced information systems, Andriole and Adelmen (1995) state:

> In contrast to many important cognitive research efforts, we do not focus on the cognitive engineering of the user interface for the sole purpose of better using a software package, such as a text editor (Card, Moran, Newell, 1983), a word processor (Norman, 1986), or a spreadsheet (Olson & Nilsen, 1987). Instead our focus is on enhancing organizational problem solving, that is, on designing the user interface to advanced information systems so that they improve our ability to perform the complex inference and decision-making tasks found in organizational settings.... "Cognitive engineering is about human behavior in complex worlds." (pp. 10–11)

As an example of their approach to interface design, we will look at a few of the items and recommendations from these authors' analysis of memory and attention. Memory consists of long- and short-term components. Short- term memory is where information is still being processed in some manner. Short-term memory is limited in its capacity for storage. Thus, the shorter the message the better. Perception and memory are selective, and one tends to remember something that can be associated with what is already held in memory. Displays thus ought to be structured to aid integration of new information within existing memory structures and across other interfaces. People are more likely to remember concrete versus abstract information and information presented in more than one sensory channel. Finally, it is easier to recognize than to recall; "Therefore, interfaces should be designed to facilitate recognition, not recall" (p. 196). This is an important study because it includes the organizational and distributed aspects of learning that LCD must ultimately deal with, especially in the design of workspaces, where more and more problem solving is based on the collaborative process.

Ehrlich (1996): Models of Human-Computer Interaction

Ehrlich (1996) wrote that though there has been much interest in mental models within the HCI community, there has not been much mental model material actually applied to the design of interfaces beyond evaluation. In exploring the possibility of applying what we know about mental models, she first defined the myriad terms that have been used in the literature (Card & Moran, 1986; Norman, 1986):

- *Design* or *System Model*—the implementor's model of the system; the conceptualization of the system held by the designer

- *User's Model*—the user's model of the system; the conceptual model constructed by the user in interacting with the system

- *System Image*—the "look and feel" of the system, its appearance and behavior; the physical image of the system

Erlich then reviewed some of the basic research on models of the user in human-computer interaction, focusing on the GOMS model of Newell and Card (1985) as a typical example of the information-processing approach.

> The GOMS model seeks to explain and predict human-computer interaction through a model of a set of tasks performed by a skilled computer user:
>
> - *Goals*
> - *Operators* or actions belonging to the user skill set
> - *Methods*—sequences of subgoals and operators often carried out in automatic fashion
> - *Selection* rules—for choosing among different possible methods of reaching a particular goal. (p. 228)

Ehrlich contended that even though this model may have shortcomings, it has allowed designers to predict whether a system is likely to be hard to learn or hard to use or both.

Of all the models, the system image has come to dominate design considerations in the age of graphical user interfaces. As was mentioned in Chapters 3 and 4 with the work of Nielsen (1993) and Mullet and Sano (1995), there is a growing set of standards that are available to help ensure that the system image will be easy to learn and use.

If UI designers do not use a "user's model" as part of the design process, they may use a metaphor, but this has been shown to be of limited use in the functional efficacy of a mental model. The real emphasis on the use of mental models has arrived with the need to develop navigation schemes in hierarchical help and hypertext systems (see next section for a discussion of hypertext and cognition). Ehrlich (1996) found in her research into users' success with sequential and hyperlinked help systems, that those who could visualize the system had more success with it (we discuss the need for explicit visualization techniques in Chapter 7). The results of her visualization and interaction studies suggested the following about users' mental models:

- The ability to visualize is not correlated with computer knowledge.

- There is a visual or spatial component in the model.

- There is also an abstract model of rules for computer interaction; these rules are transferable.

- The model consists of a representation of the structure of the information.

- Even good visualizers will not have an adequate model of a complex structure.

From this, it becomes obvious that in complex information structures like a Web site or in Web-based training, it is necessary to provide visualization help. Designers need to use an abstraction of the information structure to understand and design the proper relationships within the structure. Also, it becomes clear that standards for the design of interface objects become quite important in the ease of knowledge transfer from one system to another. Ehrlich next turned to a description of a design model. For Ehrlich, a design model addresses the following:

- Representing the main concepts inherent in the software application
- Issues of system behavior
- Separation of the presentation and specification of objects
- Levels of granularity of possible operations
- Hierarchy and containment; nesting of commands

When the designer constructs the user model of the system, or the surrogate as the designer's model, he or she relies on an informed understanding of the goal, user population, and principal features of the application. One of the advances of creating a design model is that in situations of complexity, techniques can be used to make the correct actions explicit. Just what Ehrlich has pointed out will be key to the success of LCD. The use of these two models, the designer's model and the user's model, enhances the design process and helps in managing complexity because it helps to make the implicit, or covert, explicit and overt. A concern for the cognitive is essential in the modern design process. This concern is key to uncovering what must be made more visible. LCD is based on the belief that we know enough about cognition to make and use excellent models of our audiences and that it is time we started to incorporate this knowledge in the fight against unnecessary complexity.

Now let us take a look at an information design strategy that is an example of LCD in that it attempts to make explicit some of our basic cognitive processes: That is, its organization of information elements seems analogous to the networked organization of our own memories.

HYPERTEXT DESIGN ELEMENTS

Hypertext is information that is organized in a network composed of nodes of information with links expressing relationships between those nodes. The concept of hypertext dates back to early writers and manuscript designers, but it was Vannevar Bush who articulated a technological system of hypertext. The advent of computing technology and the Internet has allowed Bush's dreams to be realized, and hypertext/hypermedia has become familiar to all as internet and intranet hypertext technology has become widespread (Rouet, Levonen, Dillon, & Spiro, 1996).

There are three potentially successful uses of hypertext (Foltz, 1996). First, hypertext can be successful as a search engine, especially for large, complex amounts of text. Hypertext's ability to navigate among relevant pieces of information is unmatched in paper versions of texts. Such flexibility in hypertext is essential in that it automatically provides cues within the presented information. These cues provide an immediate link to related information, allowing the reader's attention not to be broken by the presentation tool. Having to stop and focus on navigating a presentation tool for related information could distract the reader/user from the subject matter of the text (Foltz, 1996).

The second potentially successful use of hypertext is in representing textual information that is not easily presented in linear form. Examples of such information would be legal argumentation, help systems, or design knowledge, all of which have highly interrelated nodes of information that can be easily displayed through links, providing coherent navigation through complex information. Coherence in text means that text components share "semantic relatedness," or meaning. Successful navigation of complex information requires the existence of meaningful coherence cues. This means that the writer or information designer must determine relationships among all information pieces and structure the information accordingly (Foltz, 1996).

The third potential use of hypertext, and the most significant, lies in the fact that it provides dynamic coherence. Dynamic coherence provides additional information to the reader so that the text automatically contains information that is more appropriate to the reader's representation of the text (Foltz, 1996). Dynamic coherence provides flexibility for the reader; background information regarding the subject and instructions for navigating information can be made available for novice users or those unfamiliar with the text's content. For readers wanting general overview information, a prescribed order or single path can fill the reader's needs. For those wanting more specific or more detailed information, search capabilities or intricate linking structures can provide varied levels of detail, depending on the reader's goals (Foltz, 1996, p. 132).

Such powerful uses of hypertext can allow designers to build a single system that meets the needs of a variety of users, including novices and experts alike. The literature suggests that much theory coming from presenting textual information can be applied to hypertext. For example, theory on text processing shows that "comprehension relies ... on the reader's knowledge of typical text structures" (Esperet, 1996, p. 153). Other traditional, "linear" text theory says that, cognitively, when processing information, readers must access different information units from long-term memory in order to build up a coherent cognitive representation of the conceptual domain (Esperet, 1996). The same applies to users of hypertext.

In addition, new theory unique to hypertext will need to be developed. Initially, hypertext users must develop new strategies for reading and comprehending unique hypertext features supported by the design of the hypertext system itself. Designers of hypertext must define information units, provide interconnected relationships among those units, and "provide top-level representations to facilitate user navigation" (Esperet, 1996, p. 154). All of these are basic categorization (see Chapter 6) and visualization skills (see Chapter 7) applied to information design. Designers of hypertext can benefit from familiarizing themselves with the basic framework of reader-document interaction. Document usage or reading involves a reader defining a goal, scanning words on a page, applying a representational model of the text's structures, and manipulating the information space to achieve a certain goal.

A typical reader's framework includes the primary components of reading:

> A Task Model (T) that deals with the reader's needs and uses for the material; An Information Model (I) that provides a model of the information space; A set of manipulation skills and facilities (M) that support physical use of the material; and A Standard Reading Processor (S) that represents the cognitive and perceptual processing involved in reading words and sentences. (Dillon, 1996, p. 36)

Designers can use this model (a) as a checklist to consider all the important elements of text being designed, (b) as a design guide to deal with issues within the conceptualizing stage, and (c) to organize the design process as a whole. This framework enables the prediction of a reader's competency with documents and can also help evaluate existing designs (Dillon, 1996). Hypertext information must show relationships among interconnected information, which requires advanced preparation by the designers of the system. Designers must know their users and build a system that meets their reader's needs.

In conclusion, because widespread use of online hypertext is so new, theories regarding its design and use are sparse. However, borrowing similar work from other disciplines may provide useful guidelines in designing hypertext systems. For example, Nielsen (1993) and Guillemette (1989) have created usability parameters for other areas that apply to hypertext systems as well. Guillemette's usability factors from his studies on reading documentation are: credibility, demonstrative (precise, conclusive), fitness (relevant), personal affect (varied or monotonous), systematic arrangement, task relevance, and understandability (clear, readable, understandable). We can see that many of these elements are directly applicable to hypertext design and in turn to LCD. It is interesting that hypertext also addresses two of Soloway and Pryor's (1996) concerns for learner-centered computer-based learning systems—diversity and growth. As explained above, hypertext is particularly flexible in supplying different paths for different types of users operating at different levels of competency.

INFORMATION-FIELD DESIGN: EXAMPLES AND LESSONS

As in Chapter 4, at this point we present some examples of powerful organizers that have struggled for acceptance due to difficult learning curves, initial complexity, or simply being ahead of their time. Our first example, Augment, was about 20 years ahead of its time.

Augment—Open Hyperdoc System

This forerunner of the Web and the use of intranets was designed by Doug Engelbart (inventor of the mouse and windowing systems) in the 1970s and is only today getting the attention that it deserves. This system not only creates links between universal resource locators (URLs) but can identify and cross-link to the sentence, word, and character level. This makes it much more powerful than the current Web paradigm in identifying relevant associations. It is thus more closely aligned with our natural ability to cross-link related items from one mental model or frame to another. Besides being ahead of its time, its power naturally led to a more complex interface. The system is very sophisticated, and a significant commitment is required to learn how to operate it. It is implemented as a command-based system, but an advanced graphical user interface has also been designed for it. There are, of course, two phases where one looks for design help in working with the interface to any application: ease of learning and ease of using. Once learned, the Augment system is like flying at 30,000 feet over the information produced within an organization—unobstructed, smooth, powerful, and flexible. Without reducing the cost of learning, the system still finds a bit of a barrier to broad acceptance, much like the very sophisticated yet hard-to-learn cataloging system called PRECIS, which is discussed in Chapter 6. But it is quite clear that Augment's real barrier to acceptance was that it was invented ahead of our understanding of the usefulness of such a hyperdoc system. Today, with the revolution of the Web all around us, we know what Engelbart knew 26 years ago. However, as with the Bloomberg system, as users see a competitive advantage in using such a system to manage their knowledge assets, Augment may still find a significant loyal following in the "organizational learning" units of corporate America.

Internet Versus the Web

Much like the almost immediate acceptance and embracing of the Macintosh interface over DOS, there was a remarkable and palpable transformation in the user base of the Internet when the World Wide Web multimedia point-and-click interface was announced. Prior to that, librarians, especially reference librarians, and academics were the largest proportion of the users of the Internet. With command-driven WAIS, FTP, and Gopher search and communication tools, the Internet languished in relative obscurity from the 1960s through the early 1990s. When the World Wide Web, mosaic interface, and HTML language were released, their ease of use, ease of creation, and ease of navigation created such widespread popularity of the Internet that it may perhaps change the face of cultures, let alone commerce and communications. Moving from the command-driven Internet to the easy-to-use Web was the most dramatic transforming lesson in the power of usability we will probably ever experience, and the lesson should not go unheeded in our push for LCD.

Design of the 1997 Ford Continental Car

This auto came out as a high-tech showcase for driver and rider customization. But having so many choices and features, it turned out to be too complicated for purchasers. The redesign of the Continental for 1998 kept much of the essence of the technology but reduced the number of choices and replaced them with a set of expected standards. Complexity can hamper a design anywhere anytime, but there are ways to build in simplicity and design out complexity: The sheer power for endless customization provided by technology is often a culprit in complexity, but standards used in conjunction with technology are often powerful sources of simplification. Remember the LCD watchword: Do not confuse convenience with simplicity. A million conveniences do not simplicity make.

REPRESENTATION AND HYPERTEXT:
MANAGING COMPLEXITY

Various aspects of the cognitive theory of mental models have great significance for the problem of managing complexity and discovering the elements of learner-centered design. Cognitive psychological theory helps to identify not only cognitive functions that may be overwhelmed by an environment of information overload but also critical cognitive functions that, considered in terms of our design scheme, may be necessary to reach understanding. The following is a list of the essential points:

- A web of knowledge relevant to understanding a topic or scenario may be represented or conceptualized as a mental model.

- Existing knowledge is that which is already held in a knowledge structure or frame network. New knowledge may be created from the reorganization of existing models or from the creation of a new structure accommodating external information.

- Information is new material that is available in the environment and considered relevant to the individual. *Relevancy* means that it may be useful in the creation or modification of a mental model according to the individual's learning goal.

- Experts are differentiated from novices most often by the organization and richness of their mental models in a specific domain (see more expert-novice distinctions in Chapter 8).

- Filtering of irrelevant information from relevant is critical.

- The ability to link relevant but fragmented information into some coherent whole allows for new knowledge.

- Having an adequate contextual knowledge base greatly enhances the possibility for the assimilation of new information within preexisting models.

- Knowledge converted from serial data into organized patterns allows for pattern matching.

- Pattern recognition reduces the effort of processing facts individually and speeds up understanding and the generalizability of insight.

- People use heuristics, or general templates, for solving problems by selecting relevant information from the totality of information available. Heuristics are often faster than serial algorithms in solving problems.

- Hypertext represents a cognitively enabled tool.

Many of the items on the list above relate to theories of learning and problem solving and even intelligence (Sternberg, 1990). Each of these points directly influences our design problem because it can be applied to learning in an overloaded situation. In our complex world, we have limited time for the processing of information, combined with a hyperabundance of available information. This means that getting to critical information, relating it to our existing knowledge, and reconstructing a framework for thinking about an issue all become crucial foundations for dealing with complexity and learning.

From these general thoughts we want to draw some design heuristic elements that will attack the cognitive complexity word-pair scales and move the ratings from left to right, from the complex toward the simple. The specific scales that the topics of representation and hypertext influence are those found under the design and metasocial and information overload sources of cognitive complexity.

Cognitive Complexity Word-Pair Scale

Table 5.2 lists the origins and elements of cognitive complexity due to metasocial forces and information overload and design.

Table 5.2.   Origins and Elements of Complexity Due to Metasocial Forces, Information Overload, and Design

Origin	Elements of Complexity							
Metasocial Forces and Information Overload	Novelty							Confirmation
	7	6	5	4	3	2	1	
	Dynamic							Stable
	7	6	5	4	3	2	1	
	Variety							Redundancy
	7	6	5	4	3	2	1	
	Disorder							Order
	7	6	5	4	3	2	1	
	Noise							Signal
	7	6	5	4	3	2	1	
Design	Approximate							Precise
	7	6	5	4	3	2	1	
	Hidden							Apparent
	7	6	5	4	3	2	1	
	Nonstandardized							Standardized
	7	6	5	4	3	2	1	
	Illogical							Logical
	7	6	5	4	3	2	1	
	Obscure							Obvious
	7	6	5	4	3	2	1	
	Unbounded							Constrained
	7	6	5	4	3	2	1	

LCD Recommendations

What is the impact of the complexity-fighting effects of representation and hypertext on the design of information-fields and our LCD guidelines focused on facilitating system competency along with content competency?

Recommendations for the Design of System Content

- Think cognitive model building. Take into consideration that users will be building a mental model of the content, as well as how the system works. Think of how you are structuring your information flow and help features in terms of facilitating mental model development.

- Think multiple model building. Use the strategy of explicitly blueprinting the designer's model, the user's model, the system model, and the system image.

- Construct text in a style that builds a consistent mental model from general foundations to details.

- Build a model with explicit associations between concepts.

- Support the induction process through consistency and constraint.

- Minimize the need for memory; use mnemonics and other aids.

- Use rich metaphors as explanatory tools for concepts.

- Provide a context for the concepts being discussed.

- Reduce content to that which is essential.

- Provide just-in-time, just-enough explanations.

Recommendations for the Design of System Use

- Think hypertext model. Use a hypertext design scheme when possible. Its simulation of the networking of mental models that naturally seems to occur as we learn gives it a tremendous advantage in facilitating understanding. That advantage should be leveraged to deliver both system know-how and system content.

- Think singular model. Design the system in such a way that it declares a certain model format, a coherent format. Avoid designing in such a way that multiple interpretations of the underlying designer's model make sense.

- Think coherency—design the system to act as an integrated whole.

- Make the hierarchy of groupings apparent.

- Group or classify like objects.

- Use hyperlinks for related screens such as Help.
- Be consistent and coherent.
- Do not distract attention to the irrelevant.
- Supply mental aids.
- Supply enough information for the user to build an adequate mental model.
- Refine tasks to minimize the need for memory or problem-solving skills.
- Give visual and audio feedback on the results of an action.
- Make a visual display of what actions are possible.
- Create alignment or affordance between how things look and the actions they are intended to carry out.
- Use choice constraint to simplify the neural load of possibilities.
- Design the system to allow for errors.
- Use standards where possible.
- Clearly mark exits.
- Provide shortcuts.
- Use visuals to demonstrate relationships.

CONCLUSION

As we have seen up to this point from a cognitive science perspective, Gestalt organization principles and problem solving, representation, and model building provide means of perceiving, searching, and storing information and knowledge in a structured format. The next necessary capability in our cognitive hierarchy is to find a way to organize all these knowledge structures as they are being developed and stored in memory. The organization process that allows us to locate related objects in memory is the process of class encoding or categorization. In the next chapter, I will focus on categorization and its information science counterpart, classification, and their applicability to learner-centered information-field design.

6

Learner as Categorizer

In anything at all, perfection is finally attained not when there is no longer anything to add, but when there is no longer anything to take away.

— Antoine de Saint Exupéry

ABOUT THIS CHAPTER

The LCD focus of this chapter is on issues of category formation for learners. This chapter includes discussions and examples from

- Cognitive science on categorization and induction
- Information science on classification and object-oriented programming

The resulting design principles are extracted and listed at the end of the chapter.

INTRODUCTION

One of the major topics of active research in cognitive science, and the next level on our cognitive hierarchy, is the problem of how individuals develop, store, and organize objects of thought through the use of categorization. Issues of application and implementation of this research are also being studied in information science. Categorization and classification appear to be very natural processes of thinking and organizing, from the day-to-day categorization of objects in the world to the creation of elaborate artificial classification schemes for libraries. In this chapter, we will investigate the cognitive basis of this natural propensity to organize, to chunk, to classify, and by extension, to create objects of our knowledge in taxonomies, catalogues, directories, the Yellow Pages, and programming schemes.

We will limit our investigation of categorization to the research that adds insight directly into the cognitive basis of classification and its application to our LCD proposal. To do this, I survey research that falls into two related domains from the cognitive and information sciences: (a) research from cognitive anthropology (D'Andrade, 1995; Rosch, 1978) and cognitive psychology, especially the study of induction (Holland, Holyoak, Nisbett, & Thagard, 1986); and (b) research from information science focused on facet classification and object-oriented programming (OOP) schemes.

COGNITIVE SCIENCE: CATEGORIZATION

Categorization is one of the initial methods we use to organize the overwhelming amount of perceptual information we are processing at any one moment. Due to sheer volume, we must use the categorization process to filter and make sense of what we perceive. Thus, categorization is extremely useful in making sense of the world and in making information searches more facile and more efficient. "For instance, rating, sorting, labeling, and encoding are general terms for categorization methods for reducing complexity and simplifying work" (Hymes, 1997, p. 1).

Categorization, as an organizational scheme, becomes one of the major defenses against cognitive complexity and thus becomes one of the major methods of managing complexity for both the cognitive sciences and the information sciences. Concomitantly, we might even define an aspect of cognitive complexity as the overloading of our ability to classify our experiences and other informational intake.

This chapter explores the cognitive basis of both categorization and artificial classification systems. In accordance with the argument of Jacob (1991), I will make a distinction between categorization and classification. *Classification* is limited to human-made constructs, whereas *categorization* refers to natural internal cognitive processes. Our focus is on evaluating the complexity management characteristics of categorization and their application to the classification schemes that are in use in libraries, the Internet, and other forms of information-fields (Buckland, 1991). The goal of this chapter is to place classification, as experienced in information-field design, on a firm basis of cognitive science principles. All this is done in order to develop a cognitively based bridge for the creation and evaluation of LCD products, spaces, and information—evaluation in terms of their ability to help manage complexity through the facilitation of the categorization process which in turn facilitates induction and learning.

For the design of future information-fields (i-fs) as learning systems or learner-centered systems, we must discover the more amenable modes of essential cognitive processes and incorporate them in lcd. For example, just as the use of hypertext in the Internet is closer to our understanding of how we naturally link and relate our mental representations, we also want to reflect in our i-fs a naturalistic view of the categorization process. This chapter begins to outline that view and concludes with some recommendations for the design guidelines.

Background: The Classical and Natural View

Howard Gardner (1985) and Roy D'Andrade (1995) presented an excellent portrayal of the development of research in the area of categorization from a cognitive science/anthropological perspective. They gave us a good outline of the cognitive-based history of the study of categories, concepts, and classifications from Plato and Aristotle, to Bruner and Rosch, focusing on the distinction between the "classical view" and the "natural view" of concept and category formation. Gardner summarizes the classical view as including the following three key elements:

1. Categories are arbitrary. They may be culturally determined but there is no natural limit to the categorization process.

2. Categories have defining attributes. All members share these attributes, nonmembers do not have them, and there is no overlap between members and nonmembers. Thus, there are no fuzzy boundaries on categories.

3. The intention determines the extension. The set of attributes determines the members of a category. Categories have no internal structure, and there are no differences portrayed among members.

To challenge this "classical" theory came the development of the "natural" theory of concept formation. This theory of categorization is more applicable to our proposed lcd scheme because it better reveals characteristics of the human cognitive apparatus that may be translated into learner-centered design principles.

For our purposes, the key player concerning natural theory is Eleanor Rosch. Rosch appears in the "third period of development" (D'Andrade, 1995, p. 246) for cognitive anthropology that runs from the mid-1970s through the 1990s. She opened up a new phase in the study of categorization and category learning by introducing a psychological theory of categorization. Rosch discovered that people categorize their world in terms of what is useful and by the similarity of an object's properties or attributes compared to another's. In her terms, the "family resemblance" of objects is the basis for forming most categories in everyday life. Also, she discovered that ratings of "family resemblance" are based on typicality, or the degree to which the particular object-member is typical of the category. She also found that there were base-level categories that held object prototypes that functioned as the key junction between reason and memory, between object inclusion and exclusion. Prototypes have given way to models and connectionist networks in the 1990s, but the hierarchical categorical constructs remain. More specifically, Rosch's "natural" theory puts forth the following: (a) Categories have a structure (base, supra-, and sub-levels); (b) base-level portions of categories are primary to information processing (we use them most frequently); (c) categories do not possess distinctive defining attributes—there is a fuzzy nature to categories; and (d) there may be a physiological component to what we perceive as similar.

Terms and Concepts

Cognitive Process

There are two general categories of cognitive processes. The first is control processes, which include knowledge-based rules and procedures for the appropriate performance of cognitive tasks, such as learning. The second category concerns structural processes that allow us to acquire knowledge and apply learned rules and strategies (Estes, 1994). Categorization falls into the latter category and is the basis of recognition and other forms of structural cognitive processes. The following terms are key to our discussion of the categorization process.

Category

A category is a label for a mental model or representation denoting extension and intention or members and attributes within the category. A category may signify the representation's contents as well. Categories are a form of representation that allows for the following:

- Discrimination between different types of knowledge

- The grouping of similar types of objects

- Storage of objects in long-term memory (LTM), where they can be combined and manipulated

- Easier search and retrieval

Conceptualization

A category identifies the "entity," but conceptualization adds more. Conceptualization includes the following:

- Knowledge we have about the contents of a category
- Understanding of how it works
- Knowledge to predict behavior
- Knowledge of how the category interacts with other objects of knowledge

Instances and Prototypes

Instances are memories of a specific experience of an object or process. Prototypes are abstract images formulated from that which was found to be typical among many instances. A prototype may also be the most typical instance within a category.

Similarity, Aboutness, and Typicality

These are all terms relating to the process of identifying whether a perceptual orconceptual object is a member of a category.

Researchers point out a weakness in the use of similarity or typicality as the rule for inclusion in a category. Although similarity often plays a role in category decisions, people also appear to be able to use concepts in a far more flexible manner, largely unconstrained by similarity. Also, there is abundant evidence showing that perceived similarity between objects is quite plastic and context dependent. The key point is that the degree of similarity between a member and the category prototype is not a fixed relationship but can vary depending on the circumstances (Posner, 1990).

General Models Related to Categorization

Theories on Acquiring Categories

There are four basic theories as to the cognitive processes involved in categorization. According to these four competing theories, categories may be acquired through the use of the following:

1. *An exemplar process*—in which exemplars are collections of all the specific instances of experiencing a particular object or class of perceptions, held in memory and used to compare and categorize new instances.

2. *A prototype process*—in which a prototype is the development of one generalized idealized composite of all the relevant properties of an object or class of perceptions, again held in memory as the standard of comparison to new experiences.

3. *A classical process*—in which classes or categories are formed based on rules of inclusion and or exclusion.

4. *An array process*—in which categories are formed on the basis of similarity from the selection and unification of elements throughout memory. Categories are formed not by creating an abstract prototype, matching rules, or matching a particular instance but by matching a pattern of instances grouped by commonality at the time of comparison (Estes, 1994).

Input Into Categories—General

These are the steps that one takes in linking a perception to an existing category already in long-term memory:

1. Form a structural description of the entity in working memory.
2. Search for an existing representation in LTM.
3. Select the most similar interpreted representation.
4. Draw inferences about the entity.
5. Store information and its categorization in memory.

Input Into Categories—Specific

Categorization organizes instances. It is the process of dividing the world of experience into groups or categories whose members bear some perceived relation of similarity to each other. In contrast to the process of classification, the process of categorization does not require that inclusion in one category prohibit the inclusion in other categories, nor is membership based on a set of definitive characteristics. Similarity is the basis of categorization, but that similarity is not definitive in category membership. The process of categorization is flexible and creative in that it facilitates associations between and among entities based upon the recognition of similarities in context. In a realistic categorization process, we move through a series of compromises between categories that are too general or too specific.

Example: How do you categorize an object such as a Phillips-head screwdriver? Do you label it as a general "tool," more specifically as a "screwdriver," or very precisely as a particularly shaped "Phillips-head screwdriver?" The majority of individuals will choose a categorization level that is neither too general (tool) nor too specific (Phillips screwdriver). The majority will categorize it simply as a screwdriver. This is an example of Rosch's base-level category. Interestingly, we find that experts will categorize differently from novices. They tend to categorize at the more specific sub-base level.

Theories on Retrieval From Categories

There are three theories of how categories are accessed:

1. *Access by strength of association:* The memory most strongly associated with the stimulus is the one recalled, so rehearsal builds the association.

2. *Access by search and retrieval:* This is in analogy to a computer or the retrieval of information from a library or from a URL.

3. *Access by similarity:* Sensory patterns are matched to stored patterns of attributes according to their degree of similarity. Similarity in this process makes the past and remembrance relevant to the present. The key to meaningful decision making, then, is our ability not just to remember events of the past but to judge the similarities between the past experiences and the present in order to decide on their level of relevance (Estes, 1994).

Classification Versus Categorization

The process of classification involves the systematic assignment of entities to groups or classes according to established sets of principles.

> Classification entails a one-to-one slotting of objects, events, or properties, based upon the apperception of a core of necessary and sufficient characteristics, into mutually exclusive classes within the hierarchical structure imposed by an arbitrary and predetermined ordering of reality. (Jacob, 1991, p. 78)

Categorization, as we have discussed, allows for the "slotting" of objects in more than one class and is probably not based on conforming to a set of inclusion or exclusion rules.

Categorization: Models and Authors

In this section, I want to highlight key thinkers in categorization theory and review their contributions to the management of complexity:

Rosch (1978): Natural Categories

From Rosch's work, I have extracted the following principles of the purpose and process of categorization:

1. *Cognitive economy* as a function of category systems provides "maximum information for the least cognitive effort. Categorization allows for a perceived world structure: the perceived world comes as

structured information rather than arbitrary or unpredictable attributes" (Rosch, 1978, p. 29).

2. Category research has two major priorities: the investigation into the metaphorical structure of categories and the questions as to how categories are used.

3. Categories are processed through some form of comparison or matching, but there are also other forms of processing: verifying, searching for members with particular attributes, or understanding the meaning of a category name. Categories are also learned.

4. Categories have both vertical and horizontal components:

   • *Vertical implication:* Not all vertical levels are of equal usefulness. The base level is the most useful and most distinct, and processing of the world starts at this level. The basic level of abstraction is the level that is appropriate for using, thinking about, or naming an object in most design situations.

   • *Horizontal implication:* To distinguish different objects at the same level of categorical hierarchy, we tend to form prototypes of the most typical attributes of that class of object.

5. A prototype is defined as the clearest case of a particular class. In a continuum of classes with fuzzy boundaries, the clearest cases are able to give us the most distinction from one class to the next. Prototypical members of a category most reflect the redundant structure of the category as a whole.

For the management of complexity in the learning process, this research on categorization tells us: (a) aim at the base-level category of objects when designing an I-F unless dealing with experts, (b) the use of a consistent categorization scheme builds upon the complexity-fighting effects of categorization itself to yield significant advantages in reducing the neural load on system users, and (c) real-life categories have fuzzy boundaries relying on context for clarity; so beware of context.

Holland et al. (1986): Inference and Categories

In *Induction* (1986), Holland et al. put forward a framework for thinking about problems of inference and learning that is intimately involved with categorization, explaining that, besides chunking the world for us, induction is another of categorization's key cognitive functions. The authors viewed cognitive systems as constantly modeling their environments, with an emphasis on local aspects that represent obstacles to the achievement of current goals. Models are understood to be assemblies of rules organized into default hierarchies and clustered into categories. The rules composing the model act in accord with a principle of limited parallelism, both competing and supporting one another, while seemingly supporting the same hypothesis about the state of the environment.

Goal attainment, problem solving, or understanding often depends in part on flexible recategorization of the environment combined with the generation of new rules. New rules are generated via triggering conditions, most of which are responses to success or failure of current model-based predictions. The authors speculated that categorizations at the most specific level of the default hierarchy typically override categorizations at more general levels. They summarized their research in four basic principles:

1. Rules in competition (new rules fight to replace accepted rules)

    - Inference activity and new rule creation result from competition among rules to model one's experience successfully.

    - New or hybrid rules within hierarchical categories of the physical and social world emerge from competition between what was previously understood and new evidence.

2. Variability—People not only understand that objects in a category can be variable, but use the variability in making generalizations about categories.

3. Abstraction—Many rules and categories are abstract. It is possible to teach people rules at extremely high levels of abstraction.

4. Acquisition—The acquiring of new knowledge can only be understood in the light of the knowledge already possessed.

In conclusion, Holland et al. stated, induction is a flexible, plastic process. New information is regularly and flexibly integrated into the existing pool of knowledge and procedures. Models are generated with ease. This gracefulness in accepting new information and goals with little disruption is a hallmark of induction. Such gracefulness depends on the ready emergence of plausible but tentative knowledge structures integrating a category's relations, procedures, and expectations. This emergence, as mediated by the discovery and recombination of appropriate building blocks, must be the central theme to any theory of induction (Holland et al., 1986).

For the management of complexity in the learning process, this research on induction tells us that: (a) even with a natural flexibility in establishing temporary inferences from new data, it is difficult to teach new material that is not intrinsically similar to that already possessed by the learner; (b) it is vastly easier to extend a familiar rule system than to introduce a structurally novel one; (c) people must possess or be given rules for encoding the new rules if they are to apply them; and (d) induction and categorization are intertwined cognitive processes.

Jacob (1991): Categorization Is Not Classification

Categorization performs a fundamental function in the process of cognition. By recognizing similarities between potentially dissimilar entities, the individual is able to form theories, or models, of the environment that allow him or her to extend to new encounters the generalizations garnered from past experience. If we could not do this, "We would be overwhelmed by the complexity of our environment. Categorization, then is a means of simplifying the environment, of reducing the load on memory and of helping us to store and retrieve information efficiently" (Jacob, 1991, p. 79).

Like the classes nested within a hierarchical classificatory system, cognitive categories do not exist in isolation but are frequently combined into hierarchical relationships that include specific instances within the structure of broader or more general superordinate categories. Again, categories exist in continua without fixed boundaries and with no definitive sets of necessary characteristics.

Categorization has four functions: (a) aiding stability of mental representations, (b) determining through simple categorizations whether an entity is an instance of a particular category, (c) determining through complex categorizations membership in a complex (two or more attributes) category, and (d) forming concepts as components of cognitive states that provide an explanation of complex thought and behavior. Concepts are the mental representations of simple categories.

Categories are unstable as compared to classes. Whereas the process of classification is both rigorous and absolute in that it mandates that an entity either be or not be a member of a particular class, the process of categorization is flexible and creative in that it facilitates associations between and among entities based upon the recognition of similarities.

Barsalou (1983): Essence of the New View of Categorization

The picture that is emerging of the categorization process is one of natural categories that are fuzzy bounded and variable. This "natural" picture is clearly opposed to the classification schemes of the analytical organization of scientific taxonomy and the artificial conceptual structure imposed on the ordering of knowledge by hierarchically structured bibliographic classification systems. These classification systems have much in common with the classical theory of categories (that categories are invariant and distinct). The question for us is, Can we, by applying more natural modes of categorization, make better performing classification systems?

Sokal (1974): Classification, Complexity, and Science

In his article entitled, "Classification: Purposes, Principles, Progress, Prospects," Sokal (1974) listed the following characteristics of categorization that fit with our theme of managing complexity:

- All classifications aim to achieve economy of memory. The world is full of single cases, yet by grouping numerous individual objects into a single taxon, the description of the category subsumes the individual descriptions of the object contained within it. Without the ability to summarize information and attach a convenient label to it, we would be unable to communicate.

- Another purpose of classification is ease of manipulation. The paramount purpose of classification is to describe the structure and relationship of the constituent objects to one another and to similar objects. Secondarily, classification is used to simplify relationships between objects in such a way that general statements can be made about the classes they create.

In this way, Sokal (1974) pointed out,

> Classifications that describe relationships among objects in nature should generate hypotheses. In fact, the principal scientific justification for establishing classifications is that they are heuristic and that they lead to the stating of a hypothesis which can then be tested. (p.189)

Here we see an early connection being made between classification, categorization, and induction. Now let us look at some human-made classification systems that help to manage complexity in their own domains.

INFORMATION SCIENCE: USING CATEGORIZATION

In this section, we will discuss the anticipatory work of Raganathan and modern classification theory and the software engineering trend toward using OOP techniques.

Facet Classification Systems

Many bibliographic classification systems in use today, such as the Dewey decimal classification, the universal decimal classification and the Library of Congress classification, have much in common with categorization functions within the human mind. From a cognitive science standpoint, however, these systems also have many shortcomings. The structures are limiting, related disciplines are often separated, and it is sometimes difficult to place equivalent subjects in a hierarchy on the same level with one another. Multitopic items cannot be catalogued with precision. Because stability is a strong need with library classification, the integrity of the classification process is difficult to maintain, and it becomes increasingly difficult to expand and change classifications as knowledge grows and expands. Many classifications can be expanded infinitely by refining the granularity of class divisions and subdivisions but cannot change as new knowledge comes into being or when existing knowledge is redefined or realigned. This is an experience that those setting out to categorize the contents of the Web (Yahoo!) have quickly discovered.

Many classifications have pre-assigned schemes for particular topics. If a work does not fit into the predesigned classification scheme, a cataloguer must try and place it in the nearest appropriate place. The accuracy of this method long term is highly dependent upon all existing and future knowledge matching precisely with the classification scheme. An example of a classification system which closely aligned itself with the human cognitive process while trying to resolve these typical classifing issues is colon classification (cc).

cc was developed in the 1930s by S. R. Ranganathan, who is recognized as the foremost theorist in the field of classification. His major contribution was in the theory of facet analysis and synthesis, upon which cc is largely based. Synthesis, referring to the joining of different terms together, provides a more supple scheme that breaks up knowledge into classes (similar to other well-known classifications) but allows for the juxtaposition of multiple elements of a document within a single number scheme that can be unique for each work. Instead of having preassigned schemes for various topics, cc number schemes are developed uniquely for each document or information element. This allows for easy accommodation of new knowledge, as well as a shifting or redefining of knowledge based on the needs of the current time.

cc breaks up knowledge into main classes and breaks up each class into its basic concepts or elements according to certain characteristics called "facets." Within cc, there are also five fundamental categories that relate to all classes and provide attributes to facets. The five categories are personality, matter, energy, space, and time. When cataloguing documents, key components are identified that reflect every aspect and element of the subject content. These parts are then put together in a particular formula that has been designed for each class. It is easy in this context to allow concepts from different disciplines, that exist in a single work to be identified.

An example of a work classified within cc is "research in the cure of the tuberculosis of lungs by x-ray, conducted in India in 1950s." The concepts of research, treatment (cure) tuberculosis, lungs, x-ray, India, and the 1950s are all contained within the work. It is noted that some of these concepts are more heavily emphasized within the document than others. For example, tuberculosis is given more weight than India. The most weighted topic is given prominence in the cataloguing process, so a cataloguer might order the concepts in the following way, following specific divisions within a given class:

L,45;421:6;253:f.44'N5
L   medicine
45   lungs
421   tuberculosis
6   treatment
253   X-ray
f   research
44   India
N5   1950

Thus, CC follows the vertical implications of Rosch's hierarchical approach to categorization by identifying most strongly with contextual base-level attributes. Its independence from any overarching framework even allows for a blending of categories that anticipates the real-world finding, stated above, that we seem to develop natural categories with fuzzy boundaries.

Hymes (1997): Object-Oriented Programming Paradigm

From the 1970s, the aim of the OOP paradigm was to fight the increasing complexity of software design and development. Languages like Smalltalk and Java have given software designers the tools to fully implement the benefits of this paradigm. The OOP paradigm is a modern example of a design system that is based on implicit psychological assumptions about the way "people understand and perform cognitive operations on real-world concepts," with a special emphasis on the human categorization process. In his dissertation proposal "Classification in the Object Oriented Paradigm," Hymes (1997) described categorization as the organization of mental phenomena into things that can be considered the same: "Far beyond rudimentary cognition, people often categorize to satisfy some explicit goal set. For instance, rating, sorting, labeling, and encoding are general terms for categorization methods for reducing complexity and simplifying work" (p. 1). Hymes described classification as a categorization methodology that is applied to a set of items in such a way that the "results are preserved as a tool to simplify yet another task" (p. 1). Classification was defined further as the "process of organizing categories into a systematic structure, according to some criteria for the objects themselves, and other constraints for the desired structure" (p. 1). OOP is an instance of this special classification process. The author's proposed object of study consisted of the following four elements: (a) deliberate categories, those designed by individuals to meet some goal; (b) the object-oriented paradigm, a form of analysis that differentiates a system into a set of independent objects as structures and functions; (c) Rosch's concepts of categorical hierarchy, namely supra-, base-, and subcategories; and (d) Gelman's scheme of natural, artifact, and artificial categories. In the author's description, object-oriented classes are a type of deliberate (designer-made or artificial) category with four characteristics that have counterparts in cognitive psychology: encapsulation (oop) and identity (oop), seen as extensions of the cognitive processes of identification and categorization; classification (oop), seen as an extension of concept formation and categorization; inheritance (oop), seen as extensions of inference and induction; and polymorphism (oop), seen as an extension of analogical reasoning.

With these associations between the design tasks and our natural cognitive processes, it is proposed that the resulting design based on oop will reduce the complexity of software development. In other words, (a) thinking about the design of a system will be easier because the design process follows the manner in which humans naturally make sense of things, (b) maintenance of code will be similarly facilitated, and (c) with the development of reusable object-class libraries, code is available to be used to solve similar or otherwise relevant problems. The analogy to human cognitive function is not perfect: For example, most human categories seem to be fuzzy, and boundaries of concepts in oop need to be absolute. However, software development is in need of a method to reduce cognitive complexity, or cognitive load, on its programmers' short- and long-term memory. So even though this system may not be perfectly analogous to natural human thinking, it does take steps toward managing the complexity of the software development process with its focus on reusability and our natural tendency to think about the world and to reason using categories.

CATEGORIZATION AND CLASSIFICATION:
MANAGING COMPLEXITY

The potential of categorization to manage some of the sources of cognitive complexity in the complexity word-scales and thus in LCD is significant. First, categorization is linked to the inductive learning processes of creating hypotheses and forming generalizations and thus is linked directly with manipulating internal mental models. Second, it manages complexity through its pure chunking organizational ability, and it refines hierarchies of categories into baseline, supraordinate, and subordinate structures that are easy and effective to emulate in artificial systems. As with the other topics in our series, categorization does not alone manage the cognitive complexity of infor-mation-fields, but its use is essential.

Categorization leads to the immediate notion that systems, from the Library of Congress to local intranets, need to have a management strategy in place for organizing the "islands" of discrete information that accumulate so prodi-giously. Following perception and representation, categorization is the next major cognitive management tool. Categorization starts with a rough cut, a rough chunking of the data of the information streaming from complex products to their users. If the system input keeps changing, there will be continued refinement of the rough cut until its usefulness has been fulfilled. As our categories change, we are changing our mental model of a "field," reconceptualizing its objects. In the management of complexity, we must also manage the complexity of the artificial classification system itself. We are always engaged in a balancing act between having too few categories and having too many categories; we are dynamically looking for the optimum. Whether we need to optimize our classification systems or not, that effort is minuscule compared to the advantage we receive from using categorization and classification to organize our world. The following is a list of methods by which categorization helps to manage complexity for us on a daily basis:

- *Heredity and association*—When one identifies that an object belongs to a category (is an instance of that category), the object inherits the attributes of that category without being specifically observed. This enriches the understanding of the new category member without carrying with it the neural load of identifying all the attributes from scratch for each instance.

- *Completeness*—Gaps of knowledge may be filled in about an object due to its category heritage. This allows fragmentary information to become more useful.

- *Access speed*—Navigating through hierarchical structures of related objects is faster than sequentially searching all contents of memory randomly stored. Think of finding a book in a library. One wants to search by means of categories, not just serially through a randomly organized knowledge base.

From these general thoughts we want to draw some LCD guidelines that will attack the cognitive complexity word-pair scales and move the emphasis from left to right, from the complex toward the simple. The specific scales that the topics of categorization and classification attack are those found under the metasocial forces and information overload and the systems sources of cognitive complexity. I list them below and add a related series of design recommendations.

Cognitive Complexity Word-Pair Scale

Table 6.1 lists the origins and elements of cognitive complexity due to metasocial forces and information overload and systems.

Table 6.1. Origins and Elements of Complexity Due to Metasocial Forces, Information Overload, and Systems

Origin	Elements of Complexity						
	Novelty						Confirmation
	7	6	5	4	3	2	1
	Dynamic						Stable
	7	6	5	4	3	2	1
Metasocial Forces and Information Overload	Variety						Redundancy
	7	6	5	4	3	2	1
	Disorder						Order
	7	6	5	4	3	2	1
	Noise						Signal
	7	6	5	4	3	2	1
	Interactive						Singular
	7	6	5	4	3	2	1
	Many						One
	7	6	5	4	3	2	1
Systems	Circular						Linear
	7	6	5	4	3	2	1
	Broken Symmetry						Symmetry
	7	6	5	4	3	2	1

LCD Recommendations

What is the impact of the complexity-fighting effects of categorization on LCD's requirements of dual competency—that is the facilitation of both system competency and content competency?

Recommendations for the Design of System Content

- Content in all areas needs to be organized according to baseline categories. This means information may be organized in a manner consistent with a hierarchical class structure based on a known set of rules with prescribed attributes.

- Organize content categories with the recognition of similarity and typicality.

- Structuring "Help" with careful attention to the categories of help topics allows for user inference and the transfer of understanding from one element to another.

- Be explicit about the categories used to organize the content of the system (enable visualization of the learning process).

- Describe or identify the categories of content in three to four different modes, using examples, prototypes, rules of inclusion, and patterns.

- Be explicit about the hierarchies of categories used.

- Note the level of the discussion or object.

- Be consistent in categories throughout the entire system and related systems.

- Label or organize classes in a natural meaningful manner (use Wurman's LATCH mnemonic).

- The four theories of the categorization process should inform our design in that information-fields need to reflect or incorporate a mix of the natural processes of categorization in humans:

  - Use examples that are analogous to one another.

  - Use a prototypical or abstract model to explain or guide the learner-centered actions where several instances are similar but not exactly the same. In other words, prototypes are useful in organizing a whole class of similar material: actions, topical knowledge, and so on.

  - Use rules or guidelines to draw boundaries around a topic, to discriminate what is included or excluded from it.

  - Use general categories as a rough organization, and then use similarity and typicality to drive relevance for decision making.

- If the natural human categorization process uses base-level categories as the entrance point for most novices and uses subordinate classes as the entrance point for the proficient and the expert, the system needs to present to the average learner at a base level. This focus allows the greatest chance of facilitating the inference and inductive learning capacity of the user. This being generally true, the system needs to grow with the learner's own development by offering more sub-base-level entrance or access points (Sokal, 1974; Soloway et al., 1994).

- The information-field must use classes of objects to facilitate inductive processes and user competence. It must present its content in a manner that facilitates general categorization and a hierarchical organization of those categories in an intuitive way. This allows the use of the learner's ability to detect similarity and distinction and to separate the relevant from the irrelevant for the task at hand: the learning and problem solving that needs to be done.

- In constructing a Web site of information, of any size, we need to begin to make a rough cut at organization to do the following:
  - Enable efficient navigation
  - Develop system proficiency

- The organization scheme must be meaningful.

- We must find the balance between too many and too few categories in the presentation of the content and the system controls.

Recommendations for the Design of System Use

- Organize guiding elements of the interface of the information-field (I-F) according to categories.

- Be consistent in categories throughout the entire application and related systems.

- Consistency allows the functions of new parts of the I-F to be deduced from their similarity to previous functions elsewhere in the information-field.

- Use similarity to form affinity groups or related groups of functions and to improve search efficiency—we want a hierarchy of similarity within each function set across the entire interactive information-field.

CONCLUSION

Gardner (1985) has stated that

> Even if issues of categorization turn out to be susceptible to a cognitive scientific analysis; even if the naturalistic view turns out

> to be fully vindicated, there will remain crucial unresolved
> questions. For classification or categorization is ultimately a
> tool—a means whereby individuals organize their world so as to
> solve certain problems and to achieve certain ends. (p. 359)

In light of the research presented in this chapter, I am convinced that categorization can be used in design beyond our traditional use of its organization strength in classification systems (see the section on Mullet and Sano (1995) in Chapter 4). I also believe that categorization is a dynamic process that exceeds the rigid interpretation of inclusion or exclusion found in the classical theory of categories. In combining these two beliefs, we can see the full use of the natural power of categorization in designing systems that facilitate induction and generalization, not only within simple categories of content and functionality but also across categories within the I-F design. This cross-consistency forms a web of interrelated hierarchical inference engines that more closely relates to our naturally flexible human pattern of thinking and powerfully facilitates both content and system competency. Can you imagine the power of categorical consistency across a whole line of varied products?

Categorization has helped us to project or induce the function of similar things, but it has also helped us to locate what we were looking for in our own set of mental models. In the next chapter, we will explore an even more sophisticated way of scaffolding the search process: visualization.

7

Learner as Searcher

People are tired of clicking hundreds of pages ... you don't remember where you went or what came beforehand or how to navigate to what you want to see.

—Mohan Trikha, President of InXight

ABOUT THIS CHAPTER

The LCD focus of this chapter is on the learner's search for relevant information. This chapter includes discussions and examples from

- Cognitive science on visualization

- Information science on direct manipulation, agents, and information seeking

The resulting design principles are extracted and listed at the end of the chapter.

INTRODUCTION

Newell and Simon (1972) often described the essence of human problem solving as a search process. Well, today's learners are faced with a major problem, and that is how to enhance their search capability itself. Modern learners, young and old, professional and novice, are faced with the constant problem of finding relevant, high-quality information. This chapter discusses how learners find information and some of the special means designers have developed to help them. In earlier chapters, we have found that when the basic elements of perception, problem solving, representation, and categorization are applied through interface design, information design, hypertext system development, and classification systems, we can not only significantly improve learnability and usability but target understandability as well. The topics of this chapter will seek to make their own contribution to usability and understandability through the scaffolding techniques of finding that proverbial needle in the haystack, but also, and maybe more importantly, by supplying a holistic view of that haystack (helping to locate information but also helping to view things in the larger context). As Wurman (1989) has stated, access is often the key to understanding. Finding that right piece of relevant information just when you need it can often make the difference between a great and a mediocre learning experience. With the tremendous amount of information available on literally any subject, it is easy to get lost—in the application documentation, the product documentation, the system documentation, the on-line documentation, the libraries of information, the Internet of information, plus bestsellers, magazines, newspapers, newfeeds, and other mass media. There have been three competing approaches to search enhancement: (a) the use of retrieval search engines and filtering search agents, (b) the use of hypertext design, and (c) the use of visual methods from direct manipulation to large-scale visualization. In our LCD context, I will focus on visualization, or the process of transforming information into visual form as the cornerstone of the cognitive work currently under investigation aimed at helping users search (or find their way in) complex information spaces. I do this because visualization has tremendous secondary benefits for learners. It not only helps in the search process but gives users an organizational overview and context that provides considerable help in understanding an information-field's information-based content. And, as Furnas (1991) has contended, it may engage special human graphical reasoning processes. Thus the study of visualization has a chance of giving us LCD guidelines related to system-use competency (usability) and system-content competency (understandability) well beyond any contribution that could be made by search engines, smart agents, or a even a passive hypertext scheme. Hypertext has undeniable cognitive benefits in organizing information and is really helpful as a search strategy in relatively small and familiar information spaces (Nielsen, 1993). Search technology and new kinds of more human-centered query systems can also make significant inroads into the management of complexity in the search of large information spaces. But for LCD, visualization is simply more applicable to the broader notion of information-field design. The exception we will make in our singular look at visualization is an overview of some systems that combine visualization with focusing-query and filtering systems. It is probably true that the best answer for search will be found in those information-fields that are of a combined design. But in our context, we are looking at search as part of a problem- solving process where understanding information is just as much a concern as locating information. For this dual goal, visualization is the current best design solution. There are other uses of visualization or visuals besides enhancing search, but we leave those discussions to Chapter 4 and Chapter 9. Now let us review the arc of the research effort in the visualization of complex information spaces and extract some general LCD principles.

COGNITIVE SCIENCE: MODELS AND AUTHORS

In this section, we will follow the evolution of the work of Furnas on large-structure visualization from his conception of fish-eye views (Furnas, 1986) to his development of multiscale diagrams (Furnas & Bederson, 1995). His work is emblematic of the research that has been done over the last decade that is just now being used in the design of a whole generation of Internet and intranet maps and visualizers, as well as in other contexts. His work also includes collaboration with other significant researchers in the field, including Nielsen and Shneiderman.

Furnas (1986): Generalized Fish-Eye Views

In many contexts, we represent what is near to us in great detail and represent what is further away only in terms of major landmarks. This suggests that certain views of information, called fish-eye views, might be useful for the computer display of large information structures such as Web presentations of text and databases. Furnas (1986) explored fish-eye views, presenting sample displays and providing an evaluation of the tool.

With computer programs, structured databases, organization charts, on-line text menu access systems, and maps, users are forced to view potentially huge information structures through a single small window. The problem with *largeness* is that there is too much to show, ranging from local details to global structural information. As a result, it is easy to get lost: that is, to find oneself in some incomprehensible wrong place with little idea of how to get to the right place. Presumably, this happens because local views have little information about global structure or about where the user's view fits in to the overall scheme.

Several techniques have been developed to deal with this problem, most notably variants on a zoom lens analogy, making available both the global and detailed view of a structure, either side by side, as with paper road maps, or in sequence. Furnas (1986) explored a different viewing strategy based on the metaphor of a very wide-angle, or fish-eye, lens. Such a lens shows places nearby in great detail while still displaying the rest of the domain, simply by showing the more remote regions in successively less detail. The fundamental motivation of a fish-eye strategy is to provide a balance of local detail and global context. Local detail is needed for the local interactions with an information structure. The global context is needed to tell the user what other parts of the structure exist and where they are located. Also, global information may be important in the interpretation of local detail.

Do fish-eye views occur naturally in the representation of large information structures? Are they ubiquitous, and what characteristics could be copied for the artificial creation of these views by information designers? Furnas discovered that people perceive or mentally visualize their worlds with a strong preference for things close to home and a steadily weakened preference as they move their thought or perception out in a radial pattern from the local to the global. In one experiment, if persons were to make a list of 10 states, they tended to list their own first, big states next, and then local states surrounding their own, and on out radially. This fish-eye radial tendency was also found in people's knowledge of corporate organization structures, in academics listing disciplines, and in news editors listing newspapers.

If fish-eye is a natural thinking process, then it might provide a good viewing interface for large structures with concentric "degrees of interest." Furnas

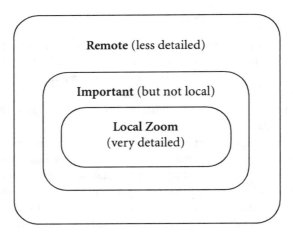

Figure 7.1.   The fish-eye scheme of organizing large information spaces into local, very detailed views and radially remote, gradually less detailed, views that provide context

concluded that this was indeed the case with fish-eye lenses but added the following caveats: (a) It is possible that viewers could need multiple fish-eye views, (b) some local views need a lot of detail because people often have an exaggerated sense of detail on the local level, and (c) there are non-fish-eye effects in the creation of natural representations of an information structure, so fish-eye preferences do not cover all of what a searcher would expect to find.

For example, a special relevancy or the increased importance of something distant may dominate over a local preference.

Furnas and Zacks (1994): Multitrees: Enriching and Reusing Hierarchical Structures

Multitrees are a class of directed acyclic graphs (DAGS) with the unusual property of having large, easily identifiable substructures that are trees. These subtrees have a natural semantic interpretation providing alternate hierarchical contexts for information, as well as providing a natural model for hierarchical reuse. The numerous trees found within multitrees also afford familiar, tree-based graphical interactions.

Research into multitrees comes from an interest in finding structures for representing information that might be richer than trees yet still viewable and navigable. Trees have a long history in representing information, from the Dewey decimal system, to tables of contents of books, to on-line information systems and electronic document delivery systems. Trees have many strengths. They are laid out nicely in the plane, and they allow simple complete traversal algorithms, they offer a natural analogue for the semantic notions of abstraction and aggregation. Trees also have weaknesses. They allow only one way to get from one node to another, so there can be no shortcuts, no alternative organizations. In contrast, general graphs often used in hypertext systems have complementary strengths and weaknesses. They allow many routes between things—cross-references, multiple organizing contexts, and so on—but the structures are not easily laid out, users are easily lost, and abstraction is not well represented. Somewhere between tree structures and general graphs are DAG, whose directed links are constrained to have no cycles. DAG were proposed a decade ago as an alternative information access mechanism. Like trees, the more general DAG can represent semantic notions of abstraction: classes above subclasses, aggregations above subparts. For information access, these structures support top-down search strategies such as trees, a natural orientation, and abstraction mechanism. One problem with DAG is that they are somewhat unconstrained. They can be difficult to lay out and comprehend. The purpose of the investigation into multitrees is to find a view of information that exists somewhere between graphs and trees. Trees have the advantage of comparative comprehensibility, viewability, and navigability. However, big trees defy smaller views and customizability.

Multitree structures are not trees, but the descendent of every node is a tree. Thus, familiar tree presentation and navigation techniques may be used to view large fragments of the structure. Perhaps one of the simplest examples of such a structure is when one has two trees sharing the same set of leaves or descendants: for example, the Dewey decimal and Library of Congress classification systems for books. Each node can have multiple parents and multiple ancestors. Multitrees are built for reuse. When another parent uses a node and its set of descendants, that node has been reused.

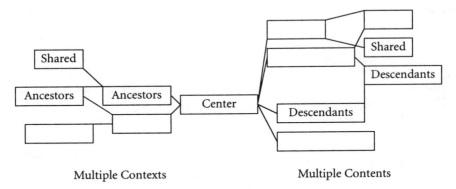

Multiple Contexts   Multiple Contents

Figure 7.2.   Multitree structure (lying on its side) showing the tree of ancestors (to the left) and the tree of descendants (to the right), with the view centered on the node called "center." Note the sharing of nodes by multiple ancestors.

Another way to think of this is that from each node its *contents* are seen descending from it, whereas its *contexts* are seen ascending from it (referring to or reusing that node). There are trees of contexts ascending from a node and trees of contents descending from each node. Multitrees thus support a special kind of browsing in its ability to navigate up, into, and across multiple contexts and down into their contents.

Fish-eye views can be embedded in multitree structures viewing the node and the downward tree of contents or viewing the node and the inverted tree of contexts, or both.

We have visited "reuse of objects or information structures" in looking at the object-oriented paradigm in Chapter 6. As discussed then, there is always a problem with reusing modules from one context to the next. For hierarchical reuse, the problem is that a new tree assembled from fragments taken from elsewhere would not hang together well. Furnas suggested two ways to get around this: (a) Admit that some points are more suitable candidates than others for reuse, and make the most use of pieces that have less external dependency; and (b) note that new trees built in the structure can introduce newly created fragments that can actually be used to clarify the new information in the structure. Furnas concluded that multitrees make a legitimate contribution to the graph-to-tree spectrum of possible structures used to represent large information spaces, combining the pros and the cons of graphs and tree structures.

Furnas and Bederson (1995): Multiscale Interfaces and Space-Scale Diagrams

As Furnas and Bederson (1995) pointed out, by 1995 researchers had spent over a decade looking for satisfactory techniques for viewing very large information structures. Central to most of the two-dimensional techniques is a notion of what might be called multiscale viewing. An interface is devised that allows information objects and the structure embedding them to be displayed at many different magnifications or scales. Users can manipulate which objects or which part of the whole structure will be shown at what scale. The scale may be constant or manipulated over time, as with a zoom metaphor, or may vary over a single view, as in the distortion techniques of fish-eye views. In either case, the basic assumption is that by moving through space and changing scales the users can get an integrated notion of a very large structure and its contents, navigating through it in ways effective for reaching their goals.

In their article on space-scale diagrams Furnas and Bederson (1995) introduced techniques for understanding these multiscale interfaces. The techniques are generally called *multiscale visualization interface techniques:* for example, zoom and fish-eye. They presented two techniques: a complex three dimensional representation and a simpler two dimensional look. The three dimensional representations consist of two dimensions of space and one dimension of scale. In the two dimensional version, there is one dimension of space and one dimension of scale. In either case, the object of the space-scale

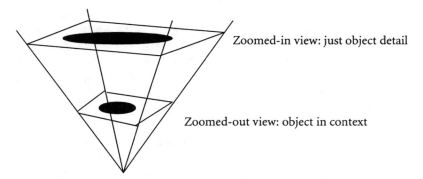

Zoomed-in view: just object detail

Zoomed-out view: object in context

Figure 7.3. A three dimensional space-scale diagram showing the different views of an object, depending on whether it is in zoomed-in mode or zoomed-out mode.

diagrams is to help developers visualize the interactions that take place among the elements of an information structure as their application pans and zooms through different size and shape views of the structure within the context of the viewing window, like a series of animation slides.

In summary, because of the popularity of Web-based information both in intranets and on the Internet, all three visualization strategies described above should be used in various applications to help people navigate these large information spaces. In the next section, we look at other approaches to the visualization and information-seeking challenge.

INFORMATION SCIENCE: MODELS AND AUTHORS

This section presents visually centered applications based on research concerning the facilitation of search and retrieval for information-system users. This section opens with the work of Shneiderman (1992) on the advantage of graphical interfaces, interactive querying, and visualization, plus a brief look at Nielsen's (1993) overview of work on managing information overload in human-computer interaction. We then discuss Kuhlthau and Marchionini's work on information-seeking behavior. As with the visualization techniques described above, the following discussion centers on computer-based information-fields, but the principles of design that we extract from these techniques will be just as valuable in the learner-centered design of non-computer-based information-fields.

Shneiderman (1992): Direct Manipulation and Dynamic Query

Visualization of information is an important concept in designing systems. A visual environment can reveal the structure of information, show its relationships, and enable interactivity, which is why "a picture is worth a thousand words." Visual representation (rather than semantic representation) is more conducive to communicating spatial relationships and actions, and it also promotes intuition and discovery. Psychologists have long known that action and visual skills emerged prior to language in human development (Shneiderman, 1992, pp. 207–208).

Direct manipulation is a visualization technique that allows a user to directly manipulate information within a system instead of using a command language. Manipulation promotes interaction between the user and the system and provides visibility of objects and actions that are of interest, as well as being rapid, reversible, and incremental. For example, in UNIX's VI text editor, one must know complex command language syntax in order to move text from one paragraph to another, whereas in a direct-manipulation environment such as Microsoft's Word or Corel's WordPerfect, one can simply highlight text and drag it to the desired location on the page.

Direct manipulation provides a representation of reality that can be manipulated (principle of virtuality). It allows the tool to virtually disappear, enabling the user to focus on the task at hand (principle of transparency). This makes it possible for the user to feel involvement with objects themselves rather than communicating via some intermediary. Direct manipulation provides visual representations of problems, which seem to be easier to retain and manipulate than textual or numeric representations, thereby enabling augmented problem-solving and learning capabilities (Shneiderman, 1992).

Examples of direct-manipulation systems include display editors and word processors, video games, office automation, databases, directories, computer-aided design and manufacturing, and more. These systems provide feedback by generating alternative actions rapidly, and they clarify structure by displaying relationships among objects (Shneiderman, 1992).

Shneiderman (1992) provided a model of user knowledge that designers can employ to build systems that are interactive and more user centered. This is important because the skills and experience of designers and their systems can be vastly different from the skills and experience of users. The model, called the syntac-semantic object-action (ssoa) model, is based on a representation of user's knowledge in long-term memory (see Chapter 5 and the description of the user's model). It is divided into two parts:

1. *Syntactic knowledge* is knowledge about how to use a computer system (we have been calling this *system competency*). It is varied or arbitrary, system dependent, acquired by rote memorization and repetition, ill-structured, and easily forgotten. This is knowledge about system-dependent details, such as how to erase a character, which icon scrolls text forward, and so forth.

2. *Semantic knowledge* is concerned with higher-level concepts. This knowledge includes both computer concepts and task concepts. Both of these categories include object and action concepts (this would also apply to system competency).

Computer-object concepts include knowing that computers store and manipulate information and include understanding how they perform such functions. Computer-action concepts include knowing that text files can be created on a computer by using such actions as loading, copying, and saving. Computer concepts are organized hierarchically, acquired by meaningful learning or analogy, independent of syntactic detail, transferable among systems, and stable.

Task concepts have both task objects and task actions. Complex task objects are often broken down into smaller units, which are more manageable. For example, books have chapters, chapters have paragraphs, and paragraphs have sentences. Task actions can also be broken down into smaller actions. For example, construction projects are broken down into a series of phases; baseball games have innings, outs, and pitches; and so on.

Putting this model together, computer users must use all the types of knowledge listed above. For example, writing a letter requires users to understand the concept of writing (task action) a letter (task object), typing the words (syntactic knowledge), comprehending that a computer will store the letter as a file (computer object), and knowing the commands to save, delete, edit, and so on. This model can guide educational system designers by differentiating the various kinds of knowledge available and highlighting which types of knowledge "knowledge users" must acquire. Direct manipulation which allows designers to "minimize syntactic knowledge and computer concepts while presenting a visual representation of the task objects and actions" (Shneiderman, 1992, p. 65).

Shneiderman suggested applying visualization and direct manipulation to current search tools and strategies (Tanin, Beigel, & Shneiderman, 1996). Intricate tools for information exploration are needed as we face more and more complex information. Successful exploration requires "powerful search techniques, more comprehensible query facilities, better presentation methods, [and] smoother integration of technology with task," (Shneiderman, 1992, p. 396). Designers are challenged in building a system that can meet the needs of new and occasional users (novices), as well as power users (experts) who use the system often and require operator refinement in their exploration strategies (see Soloway et al., 1994).

Powerful methods of information exploration such as an "improved user interface to traditional string search, database query, and index search[ing]" (Shneiderman, 1992, pp. 434–435) are currently being developed, as is the ability to query non-traditional information databases such as complex text, sound, graphics, and images. Hypertext and hypermedia are linking different information media, and advanced information presentation methods are being developed. All of these techniques improve a user's ability to reach for, successfully pinpoint, and interpret information (Shneiderman, 1992).

An example of powerful visual interfaces for database access is dynamic query interfaces (DQI). Such interfaces enable the visualization of information, which facilitates the decision-making process when dealing with complex information structures. When performing a search for information, DQI provide a visual overview of the information being searched, as well as a detailed display of the information, highlighting the information that matches the query being made. Doing this provides a visual context for the user's information while simultaneously viewing the query results. DQI provide continuous feedback as a user refines or "prunes" his or her search results by using widgets, such as range sliders, alphanumeric slides, toggles, and check boxes. This gives more control to the user in performing and refining the search for needed information.

These DQI perform their functions faster as a result of their structure and design, are easier to use, and are less prone to error due to increased user control (Tanin et al., 1996). The added advantage of using DQIs in order to visualize and understand information is that they provide powerful filtering tools and continuous visual display; they use pointing (with a mouse or some other device) rather than typing; and they have rapid, incremental, and reversible control of the query.

With DQI, we can clearly demonstrate that visualization in system design is very critical to developing LCD in that it enables users not only to build a mental model of displayed information but also to maintain a context while engaged in a localizing search. This sets up the possibility for the scaffolding of learning and the management of complexity in information-rich environments.

Nielsen (1995): The Fusion of Query and Visualization

In *Multimedia and Hypertext* (1995), Nielsen reviewed several interesting information retrieval and filtering schemes, including the University of Maryland DQI called FilmFinder, Storyspace from Brown University, and two versions of Joel Tesler's FSN, file system navigator. In our context of LCD, the impressive characteristics about these tools are that (a) they were designed with the management of complexity in mind, and (b) they integrate visualization with search engines and/or hypertext systems. Perhaps this is the best of all worlds: As one searches through an information space, one receives visual, sometimes three-dimensional feedback. Let us take FilmFinder (searching a database of films) as our example system. The FilmFinder produces a two-dimensional scatterplot of movie titles from the use of sliding scales. The scatterplot has zoom and panning capabilities (reminiscent of Furnas' work above). When a film has been located that one might like, it can be clicked on, and a hyperlink takes you to more detailed information on the movie. This information can then be used as input for a related query, chaining queries together in a progressive refinement of your film search. FilmFinder combines an interactive search interface with hyperlinks and a controllable visual display that helps you visualize your thinking process. Besides dealing with information overload, the general usability principles at work here are the "principle of letting the user know what is going on" (p. 224), the principle of keeping the user engaged with choice and interaction, and the principle of making it visual. With the use of similarity as a search parameter, we can include categorization as another cognitive usability principle at work in these "combined" systems. They are good examples of, and inspiration for, the use of combinations of cognitive principles in the LCD of all types of information-fields. What can be done in information systems can also be done in other complex products and within the context or modern high-tech workspaces.

Now let us shift gears and look at some of the information-seeking habits of learners in the process of working on an actual project.

Kuhlthau (1991): Information Seeking

Kuhlthau (1991) built a model of information seeking in which one forms a personal point of view that she termed the process of "sense making." The information search process ends, rather than begins, when people actively find meaning from information, then use it by applying it to a particular problem or topic or by adding it to what they already know about a problem or topic. Kuhlthau's meaning-seeking model has three parts: The first is physical, which includes actual physical actions, followed by the affective, which includes feelings experienced, and finally the cognitive, which includes thoughts concerning both the process and the content.

Kuhlthau proposed a six-stage information search process, as follows:

1. *Initiation:* Realizing a lack of knowledge or understanding. Feelings: uncertainty and apprehension. Thoughts: contemplating the problem, comprehending the task, relating the problem to prior experience and knowledge.

2. *Selection:* Identifying and selecting the general topic to be investigated or the approach to be pursued. Feelings: less uncertainty and more optimism, especially after the selection is made and there is a readiness to begin the search. Thoughts: weighing possible topics, thinking of criteria such as personal interest, assignment requirements, information available, and time allotted. Actions: conferring with others, initial search/skim information.

3. *Exploration:* Investigating information on the general topic to extend personal understanding. Feelings: confusion, uncertainty, doubt. Thoughts: becoming informed on topic, orientation toward information. Available actions: locating information, reading it, relating new information to what is already known.

4. *Formulation:* Identifying a topic or focus from the information processed up to that point. Thoughts: identifing and selecting ideas on which to form a focused perspective of the topic. Feelings: increased confidence and clarity. This is the turning point of the information search process, when confidence increases and the topic becomes more personalized.

5. *Collection:* Gathering information related to the focused topic. This is the most efficient time for user and information system to interact. Thoughts: defining, extending, and supporting the focus. Actions:

selecting information relevant to the topic, making detailed notes. Feelings: confidence increases.

6. *Presentation:* Completing search and preparing to present or otherwise use the findings. Feelings: relief, sense of satisfaction if search has gone well, disappointment if not. Thoughts: concentrating on culminating the search with a personalized synthesis of the topic or problem—it gets put into the user's own words. A cognitive shift has taken place.

Kuhlthau's conceptualization of an uncertainty principle in this process pointed out that uncertainty is a natural and necessary aspect of the early stages of the information search process and that it can cause discomfort and anxiety, which in turn affects how we articulate a problem and how we subsequently judge information as relevant to our search process. Kuhlthau also stated that this process is not necessarily linear. It can be iterative as one goes through an information search and further refines what one is searching for, how it will be used, and what is required—what sort of problem or need made the search necessary.

Now let us look at behaviors concerned with "on-line" information seeking.

Marchionini (1995): On-Line Information Seeking—From Browsing to Finding

The information-seeking process, like problem solving, demands a general cognitive facility along with special competencies. Total information-seeking competency consists of knowledge and skills related to the problem domain, knowledge and skills related to the search system and setting, and knowledge and skills related to the information-seeking process itself. This set of knowledge plus skills is what Marchionini (1995) characterized as the personal information infrastructure. Knowing what knowledge and skills are useful in manual environments and today's electronic environments will lead to better designs for future information systems and to better training for professionals and end users alike.

The on-line information-seeking process is both systematic and opportunistic. The degree to which a search exhibits algorithms, heuristics, and serendipity depends on the strategic decisions that the information seeker makes and how the information-seeking factors interact as the search progresses. The information process consists of a set of subprocesses. These subprocesses may default to phases or steps in a sequential algorithm, but they are better considered as functions or activities that may be called into action recursively at any time or may be continuously active in the background (as types of sentinels or daemons).

The elements of Marchionini's three parallel subprocesses are as follows:

- Subprocess Group 1—Understanding
  - Recognize and accept an information problem.
  - Define and understand the problem.
- Subprocess Group 2—Planning and Execution
  - Choose a search system.
  - Formulate a query.
  - Execute the search.
  - Examine results.
- Subprocess Group 3—Evaluation and Use
  - Extract information.
  - Reflect/iterate/stop.

Because these subprocesses are controlled by the information seeker, they most often take heuristic or opportunistic paths according to skills and experience. These paths depend on ongoing judgments about the costs and benefits of the progress being made, refinements of the task goals, and relevance judgments about the retrieval information. Electronic search systems have had a substantial impact on several of the subprocesses, especially the query formulation and examination of results subprocesses. Thus, it is important to keep in mind that highly interactive search systems and full-text databases have begun to blur the boundaries separating these subprocesses and tend to decrease the linearity of their progression. One lesson here for LCD is to stay flexible and not look at any scaffolding process as simply static or linear.

INFORMATION SYSTEMS: EXAMPLES, LESSONS, AND TRENDS

Digital Libraries Project

Related to our discussion about the general information-seeking process, direct manipulation, and visualization techniques, in 1995 the National Science Foundation, the Department of Defense Advanced Research Projects Agency, and the National Aeronautics and Space Administration funded the Digital Libraries Initiative (DLI). The goals were to advance the means of dealing with digital forms of information and then make them available via communication networks—all in user-friendly ways (Cousins, 1996). We are, of course, interested in extending *user-friendly* ways to *learner-centered* ways, so let's see what they came up with. Included in the six DLI projects are text, numerical data, visual images, sounds, spoken words, and video clips. Whereas other universities in the DLI are focusing their projects on specific kinds of data or media, the group at Stanford is working on providing the technologies for common access to the various networked sources and collections, both current and new (Cousins et al., 1996; Paepcke, 1996).

Stanford Findings

Stanford's digital library project has concluded the following:

1. Library use is part of a larger task context. Library users want to achieve goals, and library activities are only important as a means of achieving those goals. There is more to a digital library than searching, and there needs to be more to a digital library interface than a query form and a list of results. The ideal interface will present flexible task "workbenches" where users can add and delete tools, deliver information and services that support the user along the continuum of the information cycle, be persistent, and allow a user to put work down in the middle of a task and return to it later.

2. People want to get the information in as few steps as possible, so source materials must be integrated. It is not always necessary for users to understand the characteristics of individual sources. The ideal interface will integrate or keep separate very different sources with very different data structures at different stages in the information cycle.

3. People need information at the task site. The ideal interface will be mobile and will allow the user to work in different places under many different conditions.

4. Through interviews, Stanford researchers have identified five categories of information activity that recall Kuhlthau's and Marchionini's information-seeking processes: locating and selecting among relevant sources, retrieving information, interpreting what was retrieved, managing the filtered-out information locally, and sharing results with others. In general, users are involved in multiple tasks at the same time. They move back and forth among separate tasks, as well as among the five categories of activity involved in each task.

SenseMaker and Dlite

Two Stanford DLI prototype user interfaces are Dlite and SenseMaker. Dlite is a task-oriented interface. Stanford researchers developed the metaphor of work centers within the interface. These are customized for each user's task.

Behind the design of Dlite is a vision of the library as a channel to the vast collection of digital information and document services (Cousins et al., 1996).

SenseMaker is designed to help users find information both progressively and iteratively. SenseMaker users are presented with a view of their accumulated references. Within such a view, SenseMaker reduces complexity in two ways. Similar results can be bundled together, and identical results can be merged together. The choices of bundling criteria and identity criteria are relative to the type of view the user chooses, such as the author or the location of the source material. The view type serves as the organizing dimension for the display. SenseMaker users can request that features of the accumulated references be used to guide the progression from one information context to the next. Progression can entail building upon, taking away from, or replacing the collection of accumulated information references. SenseMaker users should be able to use the lessons they learn in scanning the initial collection of results to effectively build upon that collection for the next iteration (Baldonado and Winograd, 1996).

We should note that there are myriad other very outstanding educationally-oriented Web sites with digital libraries covering a host of topics. One of the most outstanding started as a CD product in 1985. The Perseus Project at Tufts is a digital library with an extraordinary collection of classical texts, art, artifacts, and architecture. It has won numerous awards for its educational approach. The Perseus overview states that the principle they follow is to use their digital capability to move between traditionally distinct disciplines such as archeology and philology. This hyperlinking capability enables our minds to transcend barriers that would normally hinder our understanding.

VISUALIZATION AND DQI: MANAGING COMPLEXITY

From these general thoughts, we want to draw LCD lessons that will attack the cognitive complexity *word-pair scales* and move certain elements from left to right, from the complex toward the simple. The specific scales that the topic of visualization addresses are those found under the metasocial forces and information overload, design, and problem-solving sources of cognitive complexity. I list them specifically below.

Cognitive Complexity Word-Pair Scale

Table 7.1 lists the origins and elements of cognitive complexity due to metasocial forces, information overload, design, and problem solving.

Table 7.1. Origins and Elements of Complexity Due to Metasocial Forces, Information Overload, Design, and Problem Solving

Origin	Elements of Complexity						
	Novelty						Confirmation
	7	6	5	4	3	2	1
	Dynamic						Stable
	7	6	5	4	3	2	1
Metasocial Forces and Information Overload	Variety						Redundancy
	7	6	5	4	3	2	1
	Disorder						Order
	7	6	5	4	3	2	1
	Noise						Signal
	7	6	5	4	3	2	1
	Approximate						Precise
	7	6	5	4	3	2	1
	Hidden						Apparent
	7	6	5	4	3	2	1
	Nonstandardized						Standardized
Design	7	6	5	4	3	2	1
	Illogical						Logical
	7	6	5	4	3	2	1
	Obscure						Obvious
	7	6	5	4	3	2	1
	Unbounded						Constrained
	7	6	5	4	3	2	1

Table 7.1.   Origins and Elements of Complexity Due to Metasocial Forces,
Information Overload, Design, and Problem Solving   *(Continued)*

Origin	Elements of Complexity						
	Expert						Novice
	7	6	5	4	3	2	1
Problem Solving	Unstructured						Structured
	7	6	5	4	3	2	1
	Many Solutions						One Solution
	7	6	5	4	3	2	1

LCD Recommendations

What is the impact of visualization on the design of information-fields and our learner-centered-design requirements of dual competency—that is, the facilitation of both system competency and content competency?

Recommendations for the Design of System Content

The content recommendations for this chapter are:

- Use visualization or visuals to display context for any content the information-field is trying to communicate.

- Provide local and global looks of information and context if the environment is complex.

- Design with consideration for our natural general and on-line information-seeking processes. This means that the right information should be made available at the right time, considering the stage of the search process.

- Make sure that an index into the information structure is available.

- Provide a map or a site map to the subject or system.

Recommendations for the Design of System Use

The basic recommendations for system use are:

- Design the interface of an information-field with the use of visual representations.

- Design using the Dynamic Query Interface strategies of Shneiderman where possible.

- Design including a visualization structure along the lines of those presented by Furnas: fish-eye lens, multitrees, or the extension of these visualization techniques.

- Design with combinations of search techniques; agents, visualization, and DQI.

- Always design necessary user actions with as few steps as possible.

- Design with the idea of allowing actions to be reversible and incremental.

CONCLUSION

Chapter 4 discussed elements of the visual. This chapter emphasized the particular value of "facilitating the view" of a "learner" into the overall structure or organization of an information space. Also, as information structures grow in size and variety of use (e.g., Web-based training systems), navigating them has proven to be increasingly difficult and limiting. New navigation schemes built on visualization techniques will be essential to the success of hypertext systems in the future. As Wurman (1989) stated

> The information explosion didn't occur solely because of an increase in information. Advances in the technology of transmitting and storing it are as much of a factor. We are affected as much by the flow as by the production of information. (p. 294)

It has been the task of this chapter to see how we can manage that flow of information and manage to keep flowing in our own performance and search for understanding at the same time.

In the next chapter, we will look at how experts use special problem-solving heuristics and review what we have learned about the organization of knowledge in expertise. We will, of course, focus our look on how the study of heuristics and expertise applies to LCD and what guidelines we can extract from this research as we continue to climb the cognitive hierarchy.

8

Learner as Expert

To design is ... to add value and meaning to illuminate, to simplify, to clarify.

— Paul Rand

ABOUT THIS CHAPTER

The LCD focus of this chapter is on issues of expertise and problem solving for the learner. This chapter includes discussions and examples from

- Cognitive science on expertise and heuristics
- Information science on knowledge engineering

The resulting design principles are extracted and listed at the end of the chapter.

INTRODUCTION

This chapter focuses on two interrelated topics common to both cognitive science and information science. In cognitive psychology, heuristics (general problem-solving guidelines) are natural problem-solving methods for deciding what sequence of steps will transform a problem representation into a solution representation (after the IPA). In a broader context, heuristics is the study of strategies for solving problems of all types. The study of expertise falls within the larger framework of the study of skill acquisition in general. The study of expertise has been used by researchers to shed light on the cognitive processes involved in skill acquisition and how those processes are transformed as proficiency is developed (Schumacher & Czerwinski, 1991). More specifically, it is thought that "underlying the development of expertise is the transformation of problem solving from a basis in serial processing and deduction to a basis in memory retrieval and pattern matching" (Anderson, 1985, p. 233). In information science, heuristics are combined with the psychology of expertise to develop programming strategies for both well-defined problems such as programming chess situations or making mathematical calculations, and more complex problem situations with vague goals, multiple solutions, and imperfect domain knowledge (Dörner, 1983). In a discussion of the typical use of heuristics in the development of expert systems, Peat (1985) described the building of one of the first expert systems for molecular design at Stanford University;

> Determining molecular structure is therefore quite different from solving a problem in logic. It is simply not a matter of setting down a few rules and then working out the results. Logic is certainly needed but the number of possible configurations could be too large, so that in real life, chemists must take short cuts by constructing hypotheses, and using their experience of similar problems to generate rules of thumb, good guesses and other forms of expert systems. …It was not sufficient to give the computer laws of chemistry. … It had to be supplied with the sort of general knowledge and expert guesswork that humans use in simplifying and solving problems. (pp. 79–80)

Peat's example illustrates the essence of this chapter: how heuristics, expertise, and thinking-process extraction (by knowledge engineers) can be used together to develop help systems for the nonexpert user. The question is, What can we learn from expertise and experts in setting up good learning environments for learners of all levels?

COGNITIVE SCIENCE: HEURISTICS

Heuristics are problem-solving, thinking, and learning tools. The challenge for us is to discover a use for heuristics in learner-centered design. My approach will be to describe how heuristics support learners in general and then to extrapolate design principles involving them. The strongest link between heuristics and design is the design of content that heuristically scaffolds users through the learning curve. Parenthetically, speaking of learning curves, note that the goal in LCD, and this chapter, is not to make our novices or professional students into experts but instead to use insights from expertise and heuristics to further our ability to facilitate all levels of topic understanding.

Terms and Concepts

A *heuristic* is a creative, yet structured way of approaching problem solving that is guided by "rules of thumb." It is a general problem-solving method that does not lead to a specific solution but guides one toward a set of possible alternative solutions. Heuristics do not guarantee that a solution will be found but increase the probability that one will be discovered. Most problems in life do not have algorithmic solutions; thus, heuristics become valuable real-world approaches to human problem solving (Dörner, 1983).

An *algorithm* is a determined set of steps that leads to a specific outcome.

Background: Problem Solving

As we discussed in Chapter 5, problem solving is a procedure in which applicable knowledge is used to move from the initial representation of the problem to the representation of the desired goal state. The basic process that occurs in problem solving is a search through all aspects of the problem (the problem space) for chunks of information (the correct operators) that can help to solve the problem (transform the problem into the goal representation).

There are four general ways of enhancing the search for a solution to a problem:

1. Following algorithms under specific circumstances

2. Following creative techniques that help a person represent the problem in a way that stimulates existing knowledge in new ways

3. Increasing the availability of relevant factual knowledge

4. Following heuristics that, among other things, help to activate memories of analogous problems and their solutions

Heuristics, rather than algorithms, meet the need for flexibility in design and will be of greatest use in our LCD protocols.

Heuristics and Learner-Centered Design

What is the rationale for including heuristics in LCD? The synthesis-oriented thinking and learning strategies of the 21st century will require great simplicity and great effectiveness if they are to be applicable to LCD and future learning systems. We cannot propose to handle complexity with instructional methodologies that are more complex than the problems they are trying to solve. They must be general-purpose methodologies flexible enough to serve a host of challenges. We cannot have a different technique for every different learning situation or information-field, for that again adds typical 20th-century cognitive complexity and spoils the efficiency of our design process. These general requirements point to the usefulness of a single general-purpose heuristic strategy (Anderson, 1985; Barsalou, 1992) for content design as part of the overall LCD scheme. So heuristics will play a significant role in LCD as a model for the framing of information-based content in information-fields.

Heuristics and Polya

Cognitive scientists Newell and Simon (1972) described the problem-solving process as simply a search through a maze that can be either simple or quite complex. This model has served as the inspiration for the more logical, rational side of the problem-solving literature (Kepner & Tregoe, 1981; Rubenstein, 1986). The other half of the problem-solving literature is more systemic in orientation (Adams, 1974; de Bono, 1970) and more representationally oriented in its creative approach to problems. In either approach, one of the primary methods of improving search or creative problem solving processes is through the use of heuristics.

If we look at the dictionary definition, there are two important aspects to heuristics in general: The term means (a) to "serve or point out" and (b) to "encourage the student to discover for oneself" (Stein, 1982, p. 622). Both of these meanings are potentially useful to our LCD scheme, but we need to look further to see how heuristics can actually become helpful. Our first topic to explore is the underlying structure of a heuristic. To uncover a typical heuristic structure, we will use Polya's (1985) well known four-stage model.

There are two basic architectural elements to Polya's heuristic:

1. A step-by-step or phase-by-phase construct. The phases are meant to progressively guide the learner toward a general picture of the solution or alternatives.

2. The use of questions within each step or phase. Specific questions are asked within each phase that are meant to help the individual visualize (encode and/or reorganize) answers that lead to the next step.

In his modern introduction to the study of problem solving and heuristics, Polya (1985) described the four stages of his heuristic approach: (a) understanding the problem, (b) devising a plan, (c) carrying out the plan, and (d) looking back. He also added other strategies to be used within these stages, such as finding an analogy, drawing a figure, looking at variations of the problem, or restating the problem. His work with heuristics was aimed at solving mathematical problems, but his principles can be applied to problem solving in general. This is demonstrated by the fact that many other authors have simulated Polya's principles in creative and systems approaches to solving problems (Adams, 1974; Checkland, 1981; de Bono's 1970).

For a reorientation on the traditional view that student cognitive activity, such as the use of Polya's heuristic, can be conceived of only as the activity of an intelligent "silo," a lone human cognitively isolated from the environment, see Pea's (1993, p. 65) analysis of the use of Polya's heuristic and the discussion on distributed cognition in Chapter 9. Briefly, Pea's "distributed deconstruction" on the use of this heuristic contended that each step of the problem-solving process is more often accomplished with the help of thinking and decision-making aids found distributed in our learning and problem-solving environments. From this, he contended that it is more realistic to include the broader picture of cognition as an interaction between user and artifact when we are designing curriculum and other learning environments. As noted above, we will discuss the useful ramifications of the distributed view of cognition and scaffolding in the next chapter.

Marshall (1995): Polya's View of Instruction

Marshall (1995) gave a mental model or schema-based analysis of Polya's use of heuristics that will be quite helpful in understanding heuristics from the point of view of "content design" and "information-field design architecture." She demonstrated how heuristics help to build mental models. Marshall took Polya's four stages and explicitly mapped them to schema development. "Understanding the problem" was mapped to the problem solver's use of identification and elaboration knowledge. For example, Marshall recommended that to begin problem solving, the solver should be concerned with a broad image of the entire problem and not with particular details. This broader perspective activates the memory and "prepares for the recollection of relevant points" (p. 124). She pointed out that part of problem solving is using what the learner already knows (see Wurman, 1997). This fact stresses the use of idiom, analogy, and metaphor: relating what one is familiar with to the new material one wants to understand. Marshall also noted that Polya's heuristic strategy is based on getting the learner to ask a series of questions. These questions are used to activate relevant aspects of the learner's existing knowledge. For example, questions focusing on understanding the problem as a whole point to identification knowledge; questions dealing with how all the information in the problem is to be used tap elaboration knowledge; questions about the decomposition of a problem concern planning knowledge; and questions about how to implement strategies that worked on similar problems involve execution knowledge. For Marshall, the goal of these questions is, clearly, to lead to the development of a schema for the learner.

Polya sought to mobilize existing knowledge to attack the new problem. Marshall mapped this mobilization to the cognitive term *activation*. She also mapped Polya's recommendation that "collecting isolated pieces of information will not suffice" (p. 125) (or that organization of knowledge is key to the problem solver's success) to the modern schema-based concept that knowledge needs to be, and eventually is, organized into an interrelated network (see Chapter 5). In summary, a mental model, such as Polya's account of learning, is "developed from prior knowledge, [is] linked through a network structure, and is capable of receiving and transmitting activation so that the network as a whole is available for processing" (p. 125) when faced with every new learning experience.

Besides the use of questions, Polya's heuristic strategy was so filled with examples that Marshall stated that his approach bordered on example-based learning. His examples are scenarios that provide information about "specific patterns, mental models, and plans" (p. 125). Marshall concluded, as I do, that Polya was essentially practicing schema-based (constructivist) instruction with his focus on identification, elaboration, planning, questions and examples, activation techniques, and an emphasis on the linking of knowledge into organized wholes, all done in the context of inquiry. We will take a further look at the efficacy of examples in the next chapter, "Learner as Student," where I present our general-purpose heuristic for "content and information flow" design. The next section describes people who are masters at using heuristics: experts.

COGNITIVE SCIENCE: EXPERTISE

Terms and Concepts

This section uses the following hierarchy of competence: *beginner* or *novice, familiar, competent, proficient,* and *expert.* This hierarchy differentiates between each level in terms of the time spent with the domain, the quantity and quality of the knowledge base, and its level of organization. Novices have small amounts of information of varying quality in a loose organization. Experts have a high quantity of highly relevant information in an intricate web of interconnections.

Background: Schema-Based Expertise

During the last 30 years our understanding of expertise has dramatically increased. Laboratory analyses of chess masters and of experts in medicine, molecular biology, and other fields have included careful examination of the cognitive processes mediating outstanding performance in diverse areas of expertise. These analyses have shown that expert performance is primarily a reflection of acquired skill resulting from the accumulation of domain-specific knowledge and methods during many years of training and practice.

Whether we are designing content for novices or for those at other levels of competency, it is helpful to understand and design from an expert's representation of a particular domain. This strategy works for LCD because the expert's representation contains the heuristics and knowledge base that are most efficient in carrying out the target activity. To set up the most likely and helpful instructional target areas for novices, we must know the categories of a topic as they exist in an expert's schema (mental model). We want to do this because experts have stripped away all the useless detail and created a very lean and essential set of solid principles simultaneously managing the topic's information overload. We will discuss extraction of expert schema elements in the next section on knowledge engineering.

This section is devoted to understanding the general elements of expertise that exist across domains. The content of this section lends itself to a comparative list format, as most of the research literature on expertise attempts to tease out the differences between experts, novices, and the other intermediate categories of competence.

Patel and Groen (1991): The Nature of Medical Expertise

These researchers summarized their discussion of domain specific expertise in medicine with a presentation of non-domain-specific elements of expertise:

- Experts have knowledge of what not to do.

- Experts know what is irrelevant or misleading information.

- Experts use forward reasoning, which depends on having relevant information.

- Intermediates (advanced beginners and competent) are not able to screen out irrelevant information.

- Intermediates are distracted by irrelevant cues.

- Intermediates formulate erroneous goals.

- Generic expertise is developed after specific expertise.

- Novices do not carry out irrelevant searches because they do not know what to search for.

- Intermediates carry out irrelevant searches.

- Experts do not tend to carry out irrelevant searches.

Scardamalia and Bereiter (1991): Literate Expertise

These authors' research was on the difference between expert writers and novices:

- Experts take more time in beginning to write.

- Experts make more wrong turns and more revisions and spend more time.

- Experts spend more effort on constructing a problem representation.

- Experts spend more time identifying and elaborating constraints, goals, analogues, and relevant principles.

- Expertise may grow dialectically: Their understanding is influenced by the interaction between the existing knowledge base and new information being derived from confronting problems.

Anzai (1991): Physics Expertise

According to Anzai's (1991) research, a person who is working on physics problems must recognize the underlying structures of the problem, generate representations appropriate for discovering solutions, and make inferences on the generated representations. Recognition, generation, and inference are the three main components of the processes in developing expertise in this domain.

SUMMARY

Research on the general differences between the representations of experts and novices reveals the following:

1. Experts use more abstract (nonconcrete) features to develop mental models of a system.

2. Expert's mental models contain less irrelevant detail.

3. Experts classify features of a problem in terms of higher-level principles in the topic domain.

4. Experts recognize common features across instances.

5. Experts rely heavily on chunking.

6. They form relations between larger chunks of the elements of the topic than novices.

7. They reason forward (rather than working backward) but will alter strategy to match a given problem.

8. Experts see more interconnections between elements; novices see categories as more distinct.

9. Experts notice complexity and overlap.

10. Experts respond more critically than novices to inconsistencies in evidence, remaining open minded to solutions longer.

11. Experts tend to take a breadth-first tack, rather than depth-first, implying a capability to visualize at the system level.

12. Experts have a deep knowledge of the basic terminology, assumptions, and concepts involved in the topic task, whereas novices tend to have a more superficial knowledge of terms and concepts.

13. Experts tend to see systemic, more holistic patterns of behavior. (Anderson, 1985; Foley & Hart, 1991; Schumacher & Czerwinski, 1991)

This rich set of implicit differences between problem solving and mental model formation implies strong metacognitive (internal monitoring of one's own thinking) awareness. This metacognitive awareness, in turn, points to the benefits of an instructional method of explicitly using select portions of thinking or information organization strategies, as described in more detail in Chapter 9. This method is designed to take advantage of what we have learned about the nature of expertise and to leverage that knowledge in the design of LCD content.

INFORMATION SCIENCE: KNOWLEDGE ENGINEERING

Knowledge engineering is a field that focuses on techniques for representing expert knowledge for use by novices. In a sense, knowledge engineers are like the information architects of the "know-how" world (Wurman, 1997). The purpose of their work is to extract understanding out of complex tacit material and to create a knowledge base that can be used (a) by programmers in the creation of expert computer systems or (b) by information system designers in the creation of training or troubleshooting guides for nonexperts. It seems obvious that the techniques of knowledge engineers could be applied to extracting and translating expertise in all subject matter as an excellent source of instructional material for novices in LCD learning systems. A knowledge engineer is often a combination of a cognitive psychologist, library and information science professional, technical writer, instructional design specialist, and perhaps computer scientist. Below is a quick outline of the types of processes used to elicit knowledge and skills from experts.

Olson and Biolsi (1991): Representing Expert Knowledge

The techniques of knowledge engineering include elicitation techniques, the summary form of the data, the analysis of the data, and the final representations of the data in presentation format. The methods are either specific or general and direct or indirect.

Direct Elicitation Methods

Direct methods rely on the subjects' reports and their ability to articulate the information being requested. They consist of the following:

- Elicitation techniques
  - Interview
  - Thinking out loud
  - Observation
  - Drawing
  - Card sorting
- Summary
  - Transcripts of the data collected
- Analysis
  - Discourse analysis
- Representations
  - Concept maps
  - Associations among concepts
  - Strategies

Indirect Elicitation Methods

Indirect methods do not rely on the expert's reports but are based on observation. Inferences and cognitive representations are drawn based on regularities in the observed results of the expert performance. They consist of the following:

- Elicitation techniques
  - Direct judgements
  - Confusion probabilities
  - Repertory grid
  - Recall orders
- Summary
  - Proximity matrix
  - Recall strings
- Analysis
  - Clustering of objects—judgments of similarity of concepts
  - Interviews used in adjunct

• Representations

   – Associations among concepts and other objects of memory

These direct and indirect methods can be combined in a cycle of discovery. After eliciting the knowledge objects in the subjects' own words from an interview, one can understand the relationships between the objects using some indirect methods. After the analysis and representation has been made, one can interview the subjects again, having them explain the apparent relationships and the strategies they used in solving particular example problems.

In summary, direct methods, such as interviews and thinking out loud, reveal some of the expert's concepts and the organization of those concepts and give some indication of their approaches used in problem solving. These methods are the basic ones used to discover expert concepts and strategies. The authors added the following caveats:

> Because they may tap knowledge about specific cases in which the investigator must induce generalities or may ask for generalities that may or may not reflect knowledge used in the expert's thinking, we recommend that the conclusions reached with these methods be confirmed with other more subtle converging measures. (pp. 280–281)

Also, the indirect methods only show the organization of concepts already identified by other means: "They show nothing about the kinds of thinking processes involved in actual problem solving" (p. 281).

When one asks experts how they knew to do this or that, they often cannot articulate how they know what they know: They "just know." For LCD, the point of knowledge engineering is that in the development of curriculum with the "instructional attitude," the designer needs to extract expertise from experts in a way that can be made accessible to beginners. The processes of knowledge engineering seem like prime candidates for this difficult task.

EXPERTISE, HEURISTICS, AND KNOWLEDGE ENGINEERING: MANAGING COMPLEXITY

The recommendations from this chapter specifically attack the complex problem-solving portion of the complexity scales.

Cognitive Complexity Word-Pair Scale

Table 8.1 lists the origins and elements of cognitive complexity due to complex problems.

Table 8.1. Origins and Elements of Complexity Due to Problem Solving

Origin	Elements of Complexity						
	Expert						Novice
	7	6	5	4	3	2	1
Problem Solving	Unstructured						Structured
	7	6	5	4	3	2	1
	Many Solutions						One Solution
	7	6	5	4	3	2	1

LCD Recommendations

What is the impact of the complexity-fighting effects of the study of expertise and heuristics on LCD and our guideline's requirements of dual competency—namely, facilitation of both system competency and content competency?

Recommendations for the Design of System Content

The topics of this chapter are concerned with two forms of content design: (a) the design of the actual content that should be included in learner-centered designed information-fields and (b) the architecture, layout, or information flow of that content. *Information flow* means the depiction or explicit linking of content into meaningful chunks and relationships. Recommendations include:

- Visualize the content broadly, as a whole, before going into details.

- Use questions as a stimulus to learning.

- Content must facilitate building on prior knowledge.

- Content and layout must expose patterns of concepts.

- Visual forms of knowledge should dominate if possible.

- Examples and scenarios should be used extensively.

- If problems are complex, focus on subgoals and link to whole.

- Exploit analogues.

- Layout must organize relevant material as a network.
- Base learning targets and content organization on expert schemas.
- Use knowledge engineering techniques to depict expert schemas.
- Do not aim to make all learners experts, but keep in mind individual learning goals.

Recommendations for the Design of System Use

- Remember to design information systems that support the expert as well as the beginner. Allow different entrance points or methods for users as they develop system competency (see Soloway et al., 1994).
- Use the expert or proficient knowledge set as the ideal, the framework to outline the contents of a training area, and then supply paths toward it from lower levels of competency. One tactic is to design in a series of iterative review modules and evaluations that can be used to position the learner at his or her current level of competency and then give him or her a road map back toward expertise at his or her own pace.

CONCLUSION

We can conclude that in learner-centered design the use of heuristics is a very powerful approach to the design of content, using both direct subject matter and a scaffolding support system. The psychology of expertise also gives us an approach to content design by giving us a target from which to work backward—that is, for supplying all levels of content, from expert to novice and from professional to beginner. This provides a design framework that allows systems such as those providing Web-based instruction to gear themselves toward the expert level and yet provide a reasonable road map for all other levels of users. It allows the system to grow with the individual. Knowledge engineering is the general method of discovering the expert know-how and "know-what" that ultimately needs to become the backbone of these systems. For example, if I am learning forecasting as a novice, I want an information system or curriculum that will understand the essence of forecasting from an expert's perspective and will scaffold me through all the details and concepts toward constructing a mental model that continually approximates that of the expert. I want to use this approach because the expert's mental model is the best organized, has made the most important connections on fact and procedure, and has already discarded that which proved to be superfluous. The expert's mental model is leanest while still being the most effective.

From learner as, perceiver, model builder, classifier, searcher, and expert, we have been building toward LCD guidelines that come directly from the learner as a reflective thinker: the learner as a thoughtful, active constructor of knowledge with the goal of understanding his or her environment. We have aimed at understanding because better understanding does lead to better performance. In this chapter we have begun this content-centered LCD discussion with Marshall's (1995) schema-based analysis of Polya's problem-solving heuristic, and in the next chapter we will culminate this effort with a look at Bruer's (1993) view of intelligent novices, a review of sophisticated thinking modes, and a discussion on scaffolding and computer-based LCD.

9

Learner as Student

I have spent much time in the science museum of my city, San Diego, watching visitors try out the displays. The visitors try hard, and although they seem to enjoy themselves, it is quite clear that they usually miss the point of the display. The signs are highly decorative but they are often poorly lit, difficult to read, and have lots of gushing language with little explanation. Certainly the visitors are not enlightened about science (which is supposed to be the point of the exhibit).

—Donald Norman

ABOUT THIS CHAPTER

The LCD focus of this chapter is on issues of facilitating understanding in people engaged in a formal learning situation: that is, learners as "students." This chapter includes discussions and examples from

- Cognitive science on intelligent novices, thinking modes, schema-based instruction, and theories of distributed cognition

- Information science on computer-based LCD, goal-oriented usability, and distributed cognition

The resulting design principles are extracted and listed at the end of the chapter.

INTRODUCTION

In this chapter, we shift gears to deal with the design, organization, and presentation of information-based content and the pragmatics of instruction and learning in information-rich environments. In other words, this chapter approaches a key problem in learner-centered design: What content (what facts, concepts, and connections) fits the constructivist model of engaged active learners, and how should it be presented (interactively, collaboratively, or passively, as in lecture)? Following Norman and Spohrer (1996), for LCD to be successful, it must be engaging, effective, and viable. The focus in this chapter is on the effectiveness of LCD, meaning, How can LCD ensure that what needs to be learned is learned? This chapter focuses on approaches to content design that best facilitate the development of adequate mental models in learners while managing their future shock (Toffler, 1970), information anxiety (Wurman, 1989), and information smog (Shenk, 1997). To address these content questions, I map a portion of Marshall's (1995) schema-based instruction, Reeves' (1996) *understanding heuristic*, Bruer's (1993) concept of intelligent novices, and scaffolding research from computer-human interaction experts to key LCD requirements.

What is the philosophy behind content in LCD? For that answer, we can apply some of the principles that are currently supporting the LCD program in the development of computer-based learning systems. What they have to say in their domain has applicability to the LCD of information-fields in general. Norman and Spohrer (1996) stated that the new approach to education that we are seeing in this century, known as constructivism or "learner-centeredness," is "somewhat akin to the user-centered focus of modern interface design" (p. 26). The focus is on the needs, skills, and interests of the learner. This is an important statement because the authors are pointing out a relationship between a belief in what it means to be human, an educational approach, and a set of design principles. That is exactly what I have been proposing for LCD throughout this book. The belief is that humans seek understanding, the educational approach is that humans create or construct understanding best with the help of just-in-time coaching. The design principles say we know enough cognitive psychology to scaffold understanding and help individuals build robust mental models of what they need to know. As Soloway and Pryor (1996) argued, "We need to address the real issue of our times; nurturing the intellectual growth of children and adults [in school and organizational settings], supporting them as they grapple with ideas ... and [in] developing all manner of expertise" (pp. 16–17). "Ease of use, valuable as it certainly is, is too limited a vision" (p. 16). Even though we are not proposing that LCD be used to develop expertise, it does have the goal of moving learners toward their own learning goals amidst the irrelevancy of the "information smog" (Shenk, 1997). It is information-based content that will make or break the effectiveness of LCD in meeting the knowledge demands and learning goals of the modern learner. With this in mind, let us examine some research on the design of content that strives to deliver understanding while managing complexity.

COGNITIVE SCIENCE: AREAS APPLIED TO INSTRUCTIONAL PRACTICE

Three functionally developed areas of cognitive study apply to our content design challenge: (a) knowledge representation and visualization, the subjects of Chapters 5 and 7; (b) a cognitive perspective on the psychology of expertise and heuristics, the subjects of Chapter 8; and (c) thinking modes, the subject of this chapter. But before we look into the modes of thought, let us put this section into context by looking at the concept of "intelligent novices" as described by Bruer (1993).

Bruer (1993): *Schools for Thought*

In *Schools for Thought* (1993), Bruer described a series of working models of the application of cognitive science research to educational practice. Most interestingly, he developed a profile of the modern learner as an "intelligent novice." Originally, he described intelligent novices as novices who learn "new domains more quickly than other novices" (p. 70) and then went on to explain why. This learner has what Perkins and Salomon (cited in Bruer, 1993, p. 52) called the "new synthesis" of skills. According to this new synthesis, learners would combine "the learning of domain-specific subject matter with the learning of general thinking skills" (p. 52) while also knowing how to monitor and control their thinking and learning. In other words, modern successful learners need to have at their command domain knowledge, general thinking skills, and metacognitive awareness to such a level that transfer of learning is efficient and effective. The question for us is, Can these things be taught, and, if so, what is the best way? Bruer described many case histories of teachers developing learning environments that do just that. The key is to remake the implicit portions of intelligence and expertise (such as thinking strategies and metacognitive awareness) as explicit parts of our curriculum. So instead of implying that students should pay attention to their own thinking and problem-solving processes, and instead of merely hoping that they will develop good metacognitive skills, learning environments should make monitoring and evaluating activities explicit and obvious to the students. In this way, students can learn what was previously thought to be unlearnable and innate. Making the covert overt and the implicit explicit will be a basic principle in LCD's view of developing effective content. Now let us look at some of these general modes of thought in more detail.

Reeves (1996): Thinking Modes

We focus here on our natural thinking modes and the development of a heuristic for designing content according to the most efficient learning aspects of those styles.

To develop a method of managing information overload, it would be mentally economic if our model were to mimic at least conceptually the natural organizational structures of our own minds. Mental model theory sets the stage for the framework of our heuristic in that the heuristic itself becomes a schemalike knowledge structure focused on learning and understanding. Taking a knowledge-engineering-like approach, the study of expertise can give us a target for the level of content we seek with the thinking modes we plan to use. On the basis of this research, we can use the power of our sophisticated thinking modes to develop a complete and broadly applicable content heuristic. What are these modes?

The creative, metaphorical, critical, systemic, integrative, and long-term modes of thinking can all contribute to the development of our heuristic and help to ensure that learning (i.e., mental model construction) develops from a rich variety of intellectual perspectives. Thus, in looking at these modes, we are doing double duty. We are looking at general thinking skills that make learners very effective, and we are looking, conversely, at how to design content using these modes that learners will find very cognitively congenial. If we are setting out to manage information overload or, more positively speaking, to develop the capacity for determining informational quality and relevance, we need to apply thinking principles that focus on that capacity, independent of any particular topic. Such thinking principles could be drawn from the following pedagogical domains (Reeves, 1996):

- *Cognitive complexity:* This is the study of modern elements of information overload and other sources of learning complexity (Flood & Carson, 1990; Gergen, 1991; Goerner, 1990; Klapp, 1986; Norman, 1988; Prigogine & Stengers, 1984; Toffler, 1970; Voss et al., 1991; Wurman, 1989).

- *Meaning theory of thinking:* It is important to associate new learning to familiar knowledge in the reading level, terms, and concepts used (Mayer, 1983).

- *Creative thinking:* This is the basis of all the other modes of learning; divergent techniques for idea generation and conceptual blockbusting (Adams, 1974; deBono, 1970); it is an absolute must in being an active constructive learner.

- *Critical thinking:* Elements of learning must include the natural and artificial use of logic—deductive, inductive, and fuzzy—as well as include an investigation of the usefulness of the general critical approach to questioning and Socratic dialogue (Halpern, 1996; Paul, 1990).

- *Metaphorical thinking:* A broadly useful learning infrastructure would go beyond logic and allow understanding of abstract and unfamiliar concepts. Metaphor and analogical thinking must be implemented as part of any comprehensive learning heuristic (Lakoff & Johnson, 1980).

- *Systems thinking:* In this chaotic, highly interactive, dynamic post-industrial-information society, any learning tool or content design needs to have a focus on relationships, wholes, and change management (Senge, 1990).

- *Integrative thinking:* This post-Piagetian form of thinking supports most of the concepts of systems thinking. Described as an adult form of thinking, it joins with reflective thinking and dialectical thinking as an advanced form of problem finding and problem solving. This newly researched field may also enhance our understanding through the process of synthesis that occurs with the integration of opposing views (Hurd, 1991; Perry, 1970).

- *Pattern recognition thinking:* Another possible source of fruitful investigation into thinking styles would come from the study of how we discover themes, patterns, and trends and how we link actions to consequences. High-level pattern recognition would be valued in coming to an understanding of vast amounts of data by identifying their overarching organizing principle (Sternberg, 1990b). As a matter of fact, it is this kind of pattern recognition that the new enterprise of "data mining" uses.

These thinking modes and some of the elements found in the next section can be used to develop the content of a very enriched model-building heuristic. My design proposal entails developing and refining a synthesis of these thinking modes into a terse and practical learning tool. Reeves' (1996) current model already gives a working example of what could be done in this synthesis effort.

The necessary capacities of any LCD content strategy aimed at schema-based learning must be twofold. First, any content design must act as a filter to focus attention on the specific information that is necessary for a particular situation. Second, the heuristic design must provide for efficient transformation of data and information into knowledge.

The following components of the Reeves' heuristic could provide a guide to the content design of our overall learner-centered design. It avoids overload by targeting high-quality, highly relevant information through high-leverage, well-tested thinking strategies. Each step of the heuristic forces an examination of a particular aspect of the topic:

- The big picture, background, or precedent, and identification of the subject is made, thereby placing it in context

- The key words in which the subject is discussed

- The basic concepts that form the foundation for understanding the subject

- The systems approach to the topic, describing the components, processes, and the relationships among them that make up a view of the topic as an integrated system

- The embedded context of the system, describing the subject's connections to other related topics

- The patterns or trends in which the described system participates (How has the topic evolved over time as a system? This combines the historical context with the systems approach.)

- The associations one can make with the subject by drawing analogies between it and what one already knows (at a higher level of competence, one can attempt to understand the metaphorical structure of the topic itself)

- A visual representation of the topic

- A critical understanding of the topic

- A theme found in the topic

In addition to supporting straightforward content understanding, design (of both content and environment) must include a scaffolding of the creative processes of divergent thinking, which support adaptability, innovation, flexibility, and collaboration. Many of the steps above, such as recognizing patterns, finding trends, creating visuals, and developing rich metaphors, are essential in helping to support these creative processes. A key in the design of I-FS—whether products, information, or workspaces—is always to recognize the fundamental productivity enhancements that will occur when the design supports our natural human creative processes.

For additional insight into portions of this methodology, I will review Marshall's (1995) work in schema-based problem solving. For the purposes of discussion in this next section, a schema is equivalent to a mental model.

Marshall (1995): Schemas in Problem Solving

As Marshall (1995) stated, "An important consideration in an investigation of schema development is the nature of the first pieces of information relevant to the schema that an individual acquires" (p. 184). She focused on two kinds of typical instructional material: "examples" and "definitions." Her research questions concerned whether examples or definitions were better at schema building—the former being considered concrete and the latter being considered abstract. Her findings led her to make the following recommendations:

- The first examples used to explain a concept were the ones the students most often used to build their schemas. Thus, first examples need to be carefully crafted, as their impact is maximum.

- If students had abstract knowledge, they seemed to use it in preference to examples.

- Both examples and abstract information together form the best instructional scenario. Abstract information needs to be included early in the learning cycle.

- Abstract learning seemed more powerful than specific learning, especially in elaboration of initial learning.

Marshall concluded that instruction should be developed to facilitate the linkage of abstract knowledge to easily understood example knowledge. It is possible that example knowledge is encoded first and then an abstract information network is built around it. After the network is built, further examples are encoded relating to its other aspects. Interestingly, examples do not seem to reinforce other examples, so using one example after another is not a good strategy.

Some further proposals of schema-based instruction also fit with our heuristic. According to Marshall, schema-based instruction does the following:

- Deemphasizes the quantity of facts

- Focuses on integrating facts that are essential rather than on acquiring more and more facts

- Emphasizes the use of knowledge demonstrated by the ability to integrate and apply it

- Is delivered in a top-down fashion. This avoids the detachment that can be found in hierarchically based curriculum design, which is often delivered in bottom-up instruction modules. Top-down instruction gives learners the big picture of the knowledge domain while they are learning individual modules. This gives learners a chance to categorize and chunk the contents of the whole domain. This is reminiscent of Furnas' fish-eye view with its local detail and general context (see Chapter 8).

- Explicitly focuses on the links between the elements of the knowledge domain.

Marshall's example of schema-based instruction coincides well with our proposed content heuristic:

- In the first phase, instruction begins with fundamental situations, ideas, and events; students are familiarized with core concepts.

- The second phase consists of a few well-crafted examples.

- In general, there is an emphasis on heuristics for planning and problem solving, where heuristics consist of a series of questions.

- The heuristics themselves should be made explicitly available to the students who will use them.

LCD and Distributed Cognition

Recently, there has been much renewed interest in the idea that cognition is not just an intrapersonal phenomenon but is in fact a constellation of ongoing interactions between individuals and their sociocultural environment (Friedman & Carterette, 1996; Hutchins, 1995; Salomon, 1993). This is a broad topic arena, but, in keeping with the intent of this book, we want to investigate how this expanded idea of cognition helps us to understand elements of cognitive complexity and subsequently helps us in developing guidelines for LCD. In looking for LCD insights from this area of study, I focus on a pattern of explanation that arises from definitions of what actually constitutes the distributed cognition experience.

Hutchins (1995) stated that

> the system of the ship navigation that he had presented was based on ... manipulations of numbers and of the symbols and lines drawn on a chart ... But not all the representations that are processed ... are in the heads of the quartermasters. Many of them are in the culturally constituted material environment that the quartermasters share with and produce for each other. (p. 360)

He went on to argue that

> the cognitive properties of the human are not the same as the properties of the system that is made up of the human in inter-action with these symbols. The properties ... produce some kind

of computation. But that does not mean that the computation is happening inside the person's head. (p. 361)

According to Pea (1993),

> Computer tools serve not as they are often construed—as "amplifiers" of cognition—but as "reorganizers of mental functioning." The distinction highlights the functional organization, or system characteristics, of human activity. ... What humans actually do in their activities changes when the functional organization of that activity is transformed by technologies. (p. 57)

Pea also went on to "consider the child-computer as the developmental unit" and asked whether computer systems could "serve interactively as adults and more able peers" do in helping to support children through their development, especially in the area of education. Here he made a distinction between "pedagogic systems" that "focus on achieving the cognitive self-sufficiency of their users" and "pragmatic systems" that "allow for precocious intellectual performances of which the child may be incapable without the system's support" (p. 58). Pea listed the following as common methods for the distributed augmentation of cognition: visualization (computer aided); guided participation, "where adults often provide supported situations for children to perform more complex tasks than their current knowledge and skills would alone allow" (p. 60); inscriptional systems or writing systems, purposefully named to emphasize their external nature; and finally situated cognition (see Hutchins, 1995), where studies have highlighted "how intelligence efficiently uses resources, drafting, or crafting the environment to achieve activity with less mental effort if necessary" and exploits "features of the physical and social situation as resources for performing a task, thereby avoiding the need for mental symbol manipulations unless they are required by that task" (p. 63).

Even more on our point, Pea spoke of "distributed intelligence mediated by design" by the design of artifact:

> What I realized [with the Logo system] was that, although Papert could "see" teachers' interventions (a kind of social distribution of intelligence contributing to the child's achievement of activity), the designer's interventions (a kind of artifact-based intelligence contributing to the child's achievement of activity) were not seen, were somehow not viewed as affecting the terms of the constructivist argument ... But, of course, in either case [the child] could be scaffolded in the achievement of activity either

explicitly by the intelligence of the teacher, or implicitly by the designer's, now embedded constraints of the artifacts with which the child is playing. (p. 65)

I would like to respond to what has been quoted here with two thoughts about LCD. First, this last statement concerning the usual invisible nature of the scaffolding effect of design goes to the heart of the argument for LCD. If design is not thought of as possibly performing any cognitive function, then designers are not going to purposely include elements that could help it act as a better "instructor" or "mentor" or as a better ally in the fight to manage cognitive complexity and help guide the user to understanding. Second, the systemic approach that is evident in the thinking of those involved in the research on distributed cognition lends credence to and supports the basic LCD contention that cognition, and thus design, extends beyond the intellectual "silo" to the interaction of people and the products, information, and workspaces in their environment. If this is so, the design implications must be learner centered. If cognition is distributed the design of artifacts in that distributed environment must carry the extra responsibility of performing the scaffolding function. Whether these artifacts are mnemonic strategies, calculators, training wheels on a bicycle, the Hubble telescope, case history simulations (see Schank, 1997), or new computer learning environments, they can and should be seen as contributing directly to the learning process as an interactive whole. In doing so, all "distributed" artifacts should be seen as LCD information-fields with the potential of communicating valuable information to their users, forming a single cognitive process, and interacting in the overall understanding process. In this sense, LCD is based on the idea of distributed cognition. For this reason, it seeks as strong a set of cognitive-based guidelines for design as a constructivist would like to see brought to bear in classroom instruction. It is in the LCD of artifacts that we can achieve a true, and more proportional, distribution of the neural load and thus of the complexity in our lives.

In the next section, we will review the recent development of LCD in computer-human interaction. Its area of investigation corresponds to the "information" portion of the field of artifacts that I have been referring to throughout this work. Its focus is on facilitating understanding by improving the scaffolding effects of computer-based learning systems.

INFORMATION SCIENCE: COMPUTER-BASED LCD AGENDA AND CHALLENGES

Soloway (Soloway et al., 1994; Soloway & Pryor, 1996) described the needs of learners in computer-based LCD, (a) understanding is the goal, (b) motivation is the basis, (c) diversity is the norm, and (d) growth is the challenge. *Growth* means interfaces adapt as the learner learns; *diversity* means heterogeneity of style and capacity; and *motivation* means engaging and helping to focus learner attention to the task. In computer-based LCD, there is the desire to take advantage of the new and inexpensive power available in computing and move from user-centered design (UCD) to LCD scaffolding. This means transcending the previous efforts of computer-aided instruction and intelligent tutoring systems and the tendency to stick with UCD as the known standard. The other challenges that Soloway identified are equally impressive. They include (a) supporting visual-style learners, (b) developing cooperative and collaborative on-line environments, (c) fading scaffolding as a student demonstrates increasing understanding, (d) developing object libraries for scaffolding code, and (e) developing LCD software development environments. He also, in speaking of computer-based LCD, made a statement that could include our broader LCD effort: If the computer is going to be ubiquitous in household, school, and workplace, "Learning opportunities are omnipresent; instructional support can be interwoven naturally and beneficially into our daily activities" (p. 18). The basis of our LCD scheme is just the same: In the design of all products, information, and workspaces, learning opportunities abound, and instructional support can be interwoven naturally and beneficially into our daily activities. With this overlap of purpose and intention, many of the guidelines that we have been developing, especially in this chapter, will apply to computer-based learning system design issues. As stated above, Norman and Spohrer (1996) were very concerned with the effectiveness of the LCD applications that they reviewed. Effectiveness has to do with content, and guidelines developed in this chapter help to outline approaches to designing effective content—content that leads efficiently to understanding or is "appropriately scaffolded" (p. 17).

Interface Design for Students

Goal-centered design, promoted forcefully by Alan Cooper in *About Face* (1995) and *The Inmates are Running the Asylum* (1999), is especially concerned with the interactive relationship between the user, the goals of the user, and the design of software applications. Elements of Cooper's interface design principles could be used to place a unique emphasis on our learner's goals. They include the following:

1. Don't make the user look stupid.

2. Don't rely on metaphors as they require too much interpretation.

3. Don't design to the structure of the software.

4. Make the design of major screens more subtle than the design of minor screens.

5. Design with one year of future technological development in mind.

6. Don't stop the user from flowing through tasks.

7. Don't send messages if everything is OK.

8. Focus on revenue- or goal-fulfilling tasks.

9. Segregate the probable from the possible in warnings and messages.

What is especially valuable for LCD in these goal-centered software design principles is that they apply to the design of interactive-information-fields in general. They aim at, and confidently attack, complexity in the user's experience of an application.

SCHEMA-DIRECTED INSTRUCTION: MANAGING COMPLEXITY

The topics of this chapter are especially aimed at managing the scales associated with the "metasocial forces and information overload" and "problem-solving" origins of complexity because these sources are most concerned with content design.

Cognitive Complexity Word-Pair Scale

Table 9.1 lists the origins and elements of cognitive complexity due to metasocial forces, information overload, and problem solving.

Table 9.1. Origins and Elements of Complexity Due to Metasocial Forces, Information Overload, and Problem Solving

Origin	Elements of Complexity						
	Novelty						Confirmation
	7	6	5	4	3	2	1
	Dynamic						Stable
	7	6	5	4	3	2	1
Metasocial Forces and Information Overload	Variety						Redundancy
	7	6	5	4	3	2	1
	Disorder						Order
	7	6	5	4	3	2	1
	Noise						Signal
	7	6	5	4	3	2	1
	Expert						Novice
	7	6	5	4	3	2	1
Problem Solving	Unstructured						Structured
	7	6	5	4	3	2	1
	Many Solutions						One Solution
	7	6	5	4	3	2	1

LCD Design Recommendations

What is the impact of the complexity-fighting effects of both schema-based instructional design and the Reeves thinking modes on our LCD s heuristic's requirements of dual competency—that is, the facilitation of both system competency and content competency?

Recommendations for the Design of System Content

By following the content design recommendations of the *understanding heuristic* listed below, one will use most of the advantages of schema-based instruction. It forms a good basis for content design in a variety of information-fields. Along with the LCD questionnaire developed in Chapter 10, I would make the following items explicit in the content:

- Identify the topic.
- Describe the big picture or historical background of the subject, placing it in context.
- Locate key words in which the subject is discussed.
- Locate a few basic concepts that form the foundation for understanding the subject.
- Describe the parts and processes and the relationships between them that make up a view of the topic as an integrated system.
- Describe the context or environment of the subject in the system.
- Identify a pattern or a trend in the topic.
- Create an analogy or metaphor for the topic.
- Visualize with charts, diagrams, and drawings.
- Hold a critical conversation by explaining the topic to a fellow student or colleague.
- Abstract a theme as a generalizable lesson or statement.
- Use examples.
- Use progressively more complex cases to move from novice to expert level interaction.
- Base design on the systemic view of the cognitive unit, artifact-human interaction.

Recommendations for the Design of System Use

In our LCD *tool kit* presented in Chapter 10, we will develop a checklist for usability based on the same principles that have been listed above for content design extended by Cooper's (1995) guidelines as follows:

- Don't make the user look stupid.
- Don't rely on metaphors alone as they require too much interpretation.
- Don't design to the structure of the medium but to the user's goals.
- Don't stop the user from flowing through tasks.
- Focus on revenue- and goal-fulfilling tasks.
- Make the design of major screens subtle.
- Make the designs minor screens more elaborate.

CONCLUSION

Marshall (1995) concluded:

> One of the most appealing aspects of schema-based instruction is
> that it has its roots in long-standing psychological and philo-
> sophical theory. It offers us the opportunity to base instruction
> on the same cognitive framework within which we view the
> phenomenon of learning and remembering. It provides a
> theoretical justification for the abundant use of examples, and
> analogies, of visual representations, of illustrations, and of
> explicit plans. Under schema theory, we become concerned not
> just with the content of learning ... but with the structure of that
> learning. (p. 127)

The stages of the Reeves content heuristic, as developed above, represent one
possibility of how a set of principles might be used to design content in a wide
variety of information-fields. It is important to note that, in this example, the
heuristic structure is also used as a framework to filter the designer's effort in
dealing with the huge volume of information that is inevitably available on any
topic. The heuristic adds a focus that helps the designer to bypass irrelevant or
extraneous information, differentiating simple information from the infor-
mative. It also takes the learner through a comprehensive set of thinking activities, that should expedite the process of learning. Thus, the content guidelines
listed above are aimed at providing a means both to cope with information
overload and to achieve a high level of comprehensive understanding. This is
therefore an example of a practical content design framework for LCD.

We have covered a lot of ground in this synthesis. We have moved from low-
order perception to high-order thinking modes, developing LCD guidelines
from each topic area, all essential in making a modern cognitive-based
comprehensive design scheme. But with all this inclusion, some important
subjects and approaches have been left out. This only points out that LCD has
the potential to affect and be affected by the broad range of current research
topics being created in the wake of the cognitive revolution. It is my hope that
the LCD scheme will become a practical and effective implementation of much
that is useful in managing the complexity of our everyday lives, making our
lives ultimately more enjoyable. The next chapter summarizes the recommendations in this book in a practical, streamlined, and readily usable set of evaluation tools and design guidelines.

Tools for Learner-Centered Design

(or, Do Not Mistake Convenience for Simplicity)

Appropriate design is a hard job. But without it, our tools will continue to frustrate, to confuse more than clarify, and to get in the way rather than merge with the task.

—Donald Norman

ABOUT THIS CHAPTER

The LCD focus of this chapter is on presenting the LCD *tool kit*. The LCD *tool kit* contains the following:

- Design and evaluation tool in a scale format
- Design and evaluation tool in a questionnaire format
- Design and evaluation tool in a checklist format

INTRODUCTION

In our mission to discover and describe a LCD method that focuses on the management of complexity and is based on cognitive and information science research, we have reviewed six productive sources in the chapters: "Learners as Perceivers," "Learners as Model Builders," "Learners as Categorizers," "Learners as Searchers," "Learners as Experts," and "Learners as Students."

From the cognitive sciences, we have discussed the following topics:

- Schema-driven learning in students, thinking modes, and distributed cognition

- The elements of expertise and use of heuristics in problem solving
- The basis of visualization and its effective use in search and contextualization
- The processes of categorization that propel induction and hypothesis testing
- Representation and the development of mental models
- The power of the perceptual process to organize our informational input using the basic elements of color and the Gestalt organization principles

From the information science perspective, we have explored the following:

- Applying principles of perception and model building to interface design
- The focus of information architects on scaffolding "understanding"
- The advantage of hypertext systems
- Our natural propensity for chunking and the creation of classification systems
- Visualization and DQI techniques for enhancing search and contextualization
- Information-seeking strategies
- Approaches to capturing expertise in knowledge engineering
- The recent developments of LCD in computer-based learning systems

In so doing, we discovered that in the design of information-fields, or product, information, and workspace artifacts, we are compelled to design toward the following:

- The natural organization of sensory perceptions
- The unity, refinement, and fitness principles of simplicity and elegance in *both* graphic and textual content
- The chunking of interrelated material in system layout and content
- The hyperlinking and visual basis for navigation and the structural arrangement of elements
- The baseline entry and hierarchical organization of our natural categorization process
- The linking of relevant search and navigation schemes with the power of directly manipulated visual representation

- The knowledge of the differences and the similarities between experts and novices and how they can be modeled and exploited for scaffolding of adaptive content

- Designing content for optimum learning while controlling factors of quality, relevance, and overload using heuristics

- Basing design on the systemic view of the cognitive unit, artifact-human interaction

I have proposed that because of the rise in cognitive complexity, as described earlier, there is a need to focus on complexity as a specific design problem. The easiest way to discover high-leverage design principles that can fight that complexity is to view the user as a learner, a cognitively based interactive problem solver with a need to understand; hence the labeling of this design scheme, as *learner-centered design*. LCD principles are meant to supplement the current best practices of existing design found in such volumes as Norman and Draper's *User Centered System Design* (1986), Norman's *The Psychology of Everyday Things* (1988), Mullet and Sano's *Designing Visual Interfaces* (1995), Wurman's *Information Architects* (1997), and Tufte's *Visual Explanations* (1997). This approach holds for both designing and evaluating information-fields. The design evaluation models I have developed are meant to supplement other current evaluatory procedures as well (Nielsen, 1992). To this end, I have tried not to reiterate the content of these other volumes except as they pertain directly to my design and evaluative scheme. The goal of LCD remains to manage the complexity of learning at the interface between the learner and the information source such that the user and object can combine to scaffold efficient and effective interaction.

In the style of distributed cognition, I have assembled two evaluation and design heuristics and one checklist of design principles aimed at managing complexity and realizing an engaging, effective, and viable LCD. What is special in LCD is the dual aim of the design: to teach system-competency, as well as content-competency. This inclusion of understandability as a main component of design depends on taking maximum advantage of the entire cognitive hierarchy. This approach, among other things, helps us to manage the complexity of the artifact interface and the distributed learning process. Finally, LCD is especially appropriate for those information systems that seek to inform, train, teach, evaluate, collaborate, cooperate, or educate; these are very special information-fields.

These evaluation and design tools and the checklist add or incorporate a specific cognitive basis to current design, with an emphasis on understand-ability and the management of cognitive complexity. Conversely, these evalu-ative design heuristics should enable one to detect the presence or absence of cognitively based principles in any designed artifact.

COGNITIVE COMPLEXITY — LCD AND EVALUATION

The LCD *tool kit* includes a series of scales, a questionnaire, and a checklist of principles. The scales are based on my analysis of the sources of cognitive complexity. The sample questionnaire focuses more directly on hindrances to effective content learning. The checklist summarizes the guidelines developed in each chapter from our review of research in the cognitive and information sciences. All instruments in the *tool kit* apply to the design of the full range of information-fields: products, information design and systems, and workspaces.

LCD Word-Pair Scales: Focus on Cognitive Complexity

Table 10.1 includes the complexity management scales. After Guillemette (1989), I propose this instrument to be used to rate the cognitive complexity of any design in terms of both its interface and its content. This is a new tool and is shown here to serve as a model of what could be developed for evaluating overall design complexity. This model contains some of the word-pairs developed in Chapter 2, covering five sources of cognitive complexity, and is thus relatively comprehensive. However, it is not exhaustive, and others may want to add ratings for physical complexity such as barriers and so on. It is meant as a model and is presented here to inspire further work in this area while it may serve as a quick and inexpensive design review module. Functionally speaking, a good complexity management design would be rated on these scales by circling the smaller numbers to the right of each individual word-pair. I propose that scoring the instrument by adding up individual ratings will demonstrate relative levels of complexity. Higher scores indicate higher design complexity, and lower scores represent complexity management. For example, in evaluating a product, one could go to the scales, observe a major category such as design, and then rate the scales in that category: Is the system laid out logically or illogically? Are standards used or not? Do entrances and exits seem apparent or hidden? Is the wording or categorization precise or fuzzy? And so on. Extended explanations for each of the word-pairs were presented in Chapter 2.

Table 10.1. Origins and Elements of Complexity

Origin	Elements of Complexity						
	Novelty						Confirmation
	7	6	5	4	3	2	1
	Dynamic						Stable
	7	6	5	4	3	2	1
Metasocial Forces and Information Overload	Variety						Redundancy
	7	6	5	4	3	2	1
	Disorder						Order
	7	6	5	4	3	2	1
	Noise						Signal
	7	6	5	4	3	2	1
	Interactive						Singular
	7	6	5	4	3	2	1
	Many						One
Systems	7	6	5	4	3	2	1
	Circular						Linear
	7	6	5	4	3	2	1
	Broken Symmetry						Symmetry
	7	6	5	4	3	2	1

Table 10.1. Origins and Elements of Complexity *(Continued)*

Origin	Elements of Complexity						
	Approximate						Precise
	7	6	5	4	3	2	1
	Hidden						Apparent
	7	6	5	4	3	2	1
	Nonstandardized						Standardized
	7	6	5	4	3	2	1
Design	Illogical						Logical
	7	6	5	4	3	2	1
	Obscure						Obvious
	7	6	5	4	3	2	1
	Unbounded						Constrained
	7	6	5	4	3	2	1
	Expert						Novice
	7	6	5	4	3	2	1
Problem Solving	Unstructured						Structured
	7	6	5	4	3	2	1
	Many Solutions						One Solution
	7	6	5	4	3	2	1

LCD Questionnaire: Focus on Content Design

In this second tool I have used the learning guidelines from the "understanding heuristic" outlined in Chapter 9 to develop a set of questions and criteria that test an information design for its ability to facilitate the development of content-related mental models.

The following questionnaire contains two parts for each question: The first part (A) concerns content-driven system usability, and the second part (B) concerns content understandability. Consistent with earlier chapters, I will use the I-F (interactive-information-field) acronym to represent the interaction of people with the products, information, or workspaces being designed.

1A. SYSTEM: Does the I-F allow the user to discover the big picture or the context: the location within the information system; the location within the procedure being followed; or the background of the tool being used? Does the design provide historical context or precedence? Does it point out relationships with other I-Fs or other relevant objects?

1B. CONTENT: Does the tool facilitate identifying the topic, giving the big picture or historical background of the subject at hand?

2A. SYSTEM: Does the I-F use language/images that are familiar to the expected user set? Does it use natural language?

2B. CONTENT: Does the system facilitate the understanding of key terms about the topics it is presenting? Does it provide the ability to define terms via a glossary or contextual help of some kind?

3A. SYSTEM: Does the I-F make apparent the conceptual foundation upon which it is operating? Is the I-F's organization scheme easy or difficult to detect? Does the organization scheme of the information provided by the I-F match the user's expectation given the context of its use?

3B. CONTENT: Does the system facilitate an understanding of the basic concepts concerning the topic it is presenting?

4A. SYSTEM: Does the I-F function in a consistent manner? Is there a pattern of operation and layout that is made visible and internally coherent?

4B. CONTENT: Is the content organized in a consistent pattern?

5A. SYSTEM: Does the I-F allow the asking of clarifying questions or dialogue? Does the system provide clarifying feedback to help guide the user?

5B. CONTENT: Does the information within the system provide critical discussion of the important issues? Does it expose its basic assumptions or answer the who-what-where-when-how-why questions about the topic?

6A. SYSTEM: Does the I-F act as a whole—as a single cohesive unit?. Can the user identify/visualize the system's components and the relationships between them?

6B. CONTENT: Does the I-F facilitate gathering information about the topics's components; describe or graph the topic's processes; explain the topic's internal relationships; and describe the topic's environment?

7A. SYSTEM: Can the user identify/visualize the I-F's major processes and or relationships between the various elements of the I-F?

7B. CONTENT: See 6B above.

8A. SYSTEM: Can the user identify/visualize whether the I-F is embedded within a hierarchy of artifacts and, if so, identify/visualize them?

8B. CONTENT: See 6B above

9A. SYSTEM: Is the organization of the I-F's interface (surface features) abstract or concrete? Is an appropriate metaphor or idiom used? Is it clarifying or confusing for the expected user set?

9B. CONTENT: Does the I-F's content supply choices of analogies to facilitate understanding for the learner?

10A. SYSTEM: Does the I-F use graphics or images to support understanding of how to use or navigate the system?

10B. CONTENT: Does the I-F use visualization (diagrams, charts) in its content to facilitate understanding?

11A. SYSTEM: Does the I-F provide different access paths for different levels of user proficiency?

11B. CONTENT: Does the I-F contain essential (highly relevant) knowledge of the topics it includes, and is this adaptable in scope to fill the needs of experts as well as novices?

12A, B: Was hyperlinking used to provide a natural hierarchically categorized information flow? Was a method of searching (engine, visualization, DQI) integrated?

13A, B: Does the I-F provide facilitation for creative thinking? Does it stimulate the fluid generation of ideas, flexibility in the types of ideas, and originality? Does it provide the requisite variety of color, shape, position, and mobility cues to remove stultifying barriers and stimulate divergent thinking, new perspectives, and new combinations of ideas?

LCD DESIGNER'S CHECKLIST

In this design tool the checklist summarizes the recommendations found in Chapters 4 through 9. It is to be added to the expert designer's existing model of best practices. This list specifically focuses on increasing system and content understandability while managing for cognitive complexity. The first set of lists focuses on understandability and the principles of content design; the second set of lists focuses on usability design principles.

Design of System for Content (List 1)

❑   As a global design principle, do not mistake convenience for simplicity; newsfeeds are convenient, but they will bring back more information to process.

Learner as Perceiver—Perception/Information Design

- ❏ Use visuals to portray complex dynamic data.
- ❏ Use Wurman's LATCH mnemonic to organize information.
- ❏ Use a sense of narrative to maintain coherency.
- ❏ Use natural dialogue.
- ❏ Break content into understandable parts.
- ❏ Use terms and language familiar to the expected users.
- ❏ Provide a context for the concepts being discussed.
- ❏ Reduce content to that which is essential.
- ❏ Progressively refine text to the most relevant.
- ❏ Present content in groups or classes.
- ❏ Ensure unity of content; avoid fragmentation.
- ❏ Visually reveal patterns in the content.

Learner as Model Builder—Mental Models/Hypertext

- ❏ Think cognitive model building. Take into consideration that users will be building a mental model of the content as well as how the system works. Think of how you are structuring your information flow and related *help* features in terms of facilitating mental model development. Content models are also facilitated by the recommendations under "Learner as Student" below.

- ❏ Think multiple model building. Use the strategy of explicitly blueprinting the designer's model, the user's model, the system model, and the system image.

- ❏ Construct text in a style that builds a consistent mental model from general foundations to details.

- ❏ Build a model with explicit associations between concepts.

- ❏ Support the induction process through consistency and constraint.

- ❏ Minimize the need for memory—use mnemonics and other aids.

- ❏ Use rich metaphors as explanatory tools for concepts.

- ❏ Provide a context for the concepts being discussed.

❑ Reduce content to that which is essential.

❑ Provide *Just-In-Time, Just-Enough* explanations.

Learner as Categorizers—Categorization/Classification

❑ Content in all areas needs to be organized according to baseline categories. This means information may be organized in a manner consistent with a hierarchical class structure based on a known set of rules with prescribed attributes.

❑ Organize content categories with the recognition of similarity and typicality.

❑ Structuring *help* with careful attention to the categories of *help* topics allows for user inference and the transfer of understanding from one element to another.

❑ Be explicit about the categories used to organize the content of the system (enable visualization of the learning process).

❑ Describe or identify the categories of content in three to four different modes, using examples, prototypes, rules of inclusion, and patterns.

❑ Be explicit about the hierarchies of categories used.

❑ Note the level of the discussion or object.

❑ Be consistent in categories throughout the entire system and related systems.

❑ Label or organize classes in a natural meaningful manner (use Wurman's LATCH mnemonic).

The four theories of the human categorization process should inform our design process. Information-fields need to incorporate and support a mix of the possible processes of category formation:

❑ Use examples that are analogous to one another.

❑ Use a prototypical or abstract model to explain or guide the learner-centered actions where several instances are similar but not exactly the same. In other words, prototypes are useful in organizing a whole class of similar material: actions, topical knowledge, and so on.

❑ Use rules or guidelines to draw boundaries around a topic, to discriminate what is included in or excluded from it.

❑ Use general categories as a rough organization, and then use similarity and typicality to drive relevance for decision making.

❑ If the natural human categorization process uses base level categories as the entrance point for most novices and uses subordinate classes as the entrance point for the proficient and the expert, the system needs to present to the average learner at a base level. This focus allows the greatest chance of facilitating the inference and inductive learning capacity of the user. This being generally true, the system needs to grow with the learner's own development by offering more sub-base-level entrance or access points (Soloway et al., 1994).

❑ The information-field must use classes of objects to facilitate inductive processes and user competence. It must present its content in a manner that facilitates general categorization and a hierarchical organization of those categories in an intuitive way. This allows the use of the learner's ability to detect similarity and distinction and to separate the relevant from the irrelevant for the task at hand: namely, the learning, the problem solving that needs to be done.

In constructing a Web site of information of any size, we need to begin to make a rough cut at organization in order to do the following:

❑ Enable efficient navigation.

❑ Develop system proficiency.

❑ Make a meaningful organization scheme.

❑ Find the balance between too many and too few categories in the presentation of the content and the system controls.

Learner as Searcher—Visualization/Information Seeking

❑ Use visualization or visuals to display context for any content the information-field is trying to communicate.

❑ Provide local and global views of task context if the environment is complex.

❑ Design with consideration for our natural information-seeking processes. This means that the right information should be made available at the right time considering the stage of the search process.

❑ Make sure that an index into the information structure is available.

❑ Provide a map or a site map to the subject or system.

Learner as Expert Problem Solver—Expertise/Knowledge Engineering

❑ Visualize the content broadly as a whole before giving details.

❑ Use questions as a stimulus to learning.

❑ Ensure that the content facilitates building on prior knowledge.

❏ Be explicit in displaying patterns of concepts.

❏ Use visual forms of knowledge predominately, if possible.

❏ Use examples and scenarios extensively.

❏ Focus on subgoals, and link to the major goal when possible.

❏ Exploit analogues.

❏ Use layout to organize relevant material as a network.

❏ Base learning targets and content organization on expert schemas.

❏ Use knowledge engineering techniques to depict expert schemas.

❏ Do not aim at making all learners experts, but keep in mind individual learning goals.

Learner as Student—Schema-Based Instruction

Use the content design recommendations of Reeves' (1996) *understanding heuristic* and Marshall's (1995) schema-based instruction as listed:

❏ Identify the topic.

❏ Describe the big picture or historical context of the subject, placing it in context.

❏ Supply key words for the subject being discussed.

❏ Supply a few basic concepts that form the foundation for understanding the subject.

❏ Describe the parts and processes and the relationships between them that make up a view of the topic as an integrated system.

❏ Describe the context or environment of the topic.

❏ Identify a pattern or a trend in the topic.

❏ Create an analogy or metaphor for the topic.

❏ Visualize with charts, diagrams, and drawings.

❏ Hold a critical conversation by explaining the topic to a fellow student or colleague.

❏ Abstract a theme as a generalizable lesson or statement.

❏ Use examples.

❏ Use progressively more complex cases to move from novice- to expert-level interaction.

❏ Base design on the systemic view of the cognitive unit; artifact-human interaction.

❏ Be explicit about the instructional approach being used.

Support creativity—adaptability, innovation, flexibility, and collaboration—as appropriate:

❏ Support adaptability—avoid functional fixedness by displaying how the information-field can be used for multiple purposes; design for maximum flexibility.

❏ Support innovation—design with requisite variety in mind to stimulate new thoughts and new combinations of thoughts.

❏ Support convenient collaboration.

Design of System for Usability (List 2)

❏ Throughout this checklist do not mistake convenience for simplicity; intelligent agents are convenient, but they will bring back more information to process.

Learner as Perceiver—Perception/Information Design

Support the following perceptual organization cues as applied to parts and wholes:

❏ Parts—of interface

- Similarity
- Proximity
- Refinement and reduction
- Fitness—supports the task
- Relationship
- Scale
- Consistency—same throughout

❏ Wholes—presentation of screen, curriculum, and so on

- Pattern recognition
- Structure—canonical grid layout
- Continuation
- Closure
- *Pragnanz*
- Unity

❏   Grouping or classification of like objects

❏   Hierarchy of groupings

❏   Coherency—system acts as a interrelated whole

Learner as Model Builder—Mental Models/Hypertext

❏   Think hypertext model. Use a hypertext design scheme when possible.

❏   Think singular model. Design the system in such a way that it declares a particular model or format, a coherent format. Avoid designing in such a way that multiple interpretations of the underlying designer's model make sense.

❏   Use hyperlinks for related screens such as Help.

❏   Be consistent and coherent (color, font, size, placement).

❏   Do not attract attention to the irrelevant.

❏   Supply enough information about the object for the user to build an adequate mental model of how things work.

❏   Refine tasks to minimize need for memory and/or problem solving skills.

❏   Supply mental aids.

❏   Give visual or audio feedback on the results of an action.

❏   Make a visual display of what actions are possible.

❏   Create alignment or affordance between how things look and the actions they intend to carry out.

❏   Use choice constraint to simplify the neural load of possibilities.

❏   Design the system to allow for errors.

❏   Use standards where possible.

❏   Clearly mark exits.

❏   Provide shortcuts.

❏   Use visuals to demonstrate relationships.

Learner as Categorizer—Categorization/Classification

❏   Organize guiding elements of the interface, of the information-field (I-F), according to categories.

❏   Be consistent in categories throughout the entire application and related systems.

❏ Consistency allows the functions of new parts of the I-F to be deduced from their similarity to previous functions elsewhere in the I-F.

❏ Use similarity to form affinity groups or related groups of functions and to improve search efficiency—we want a hierarchy of similarity within each function set across the entire I-F.

Learner as Searcher—Visualization/Information Seeking

❏ Design the interface of an information-field with the use of visual representations.

❏ Design using the Dynamic Query Interface (DQI) strategies of Shneiderman where appropriate.

❏ Design including a visualization structure along the lines of those presented by Furnas: fish-eye lens, multitrees, or the extension of these visualization techniques.

❏ Design with combinations of search techniques; agents, visualization, and DQI.

❏ Always design necessary user actions with as few steps as possible.

❏ Design with the idea of allowing actions to be reversible and incremental.

Learner as Expert—Expertise/Knowledge Engineering

❏ Remember to design information systems that support the expert as well as the beginner. Allow different entrance points or methods for users as they develop system competency (see Soloway et al., 1994).

❏ Use the expert or proficient knowledge set as the idealized framework to outline the contents of a training area, and then supply paths toward it from lower levels of competency. One tactic is to design in a series of iterative review modules and evaluations that can be used to position learners at their current level of competency and then give them a road map back toward expertise at their own pace.

Learner as Student—Schema-Based Instruction

❏ Apply the "Learner as Student—Schema-Based Instruction" content recommendations located in Chapter 9 to system usability design as well, following the example of the LCD Questionnaire. Example questions are included on some items.

❏ Identify the topic—does the I-F help identify what it is being used for?

❏ Describe the big picture and the historical context of the subject, placing it in context.

❑ Supply key words in which the subject is discussed—does the i-f define its jargon?

❑ Supply a few basic concepts that form the foundation for understanding the subject

❑ Describe the parts and processes and the relationships between them that make up a view of the topic as an integrated system—does the i-f display its parts clearly?

❑ Describe the context or environment of the subject in the system.

❑ Identify a pattern or a trend in the topic.

❑ Create an idiom or metaphor for the topic—does the i-f use an analogy appropriate to its usage?

❑ Visualize with charts, diagrams, and drawings—does the i-f use visuals?

❑ Hold a critical conversation by explaining the topic to a fellow student or colleague.

❑ Abstract a theme as a generalizable lesson or statement.

❑ Use examples—does the i-f include examples of use and functionality?

❑ Use progressively more complex cases to scaffold the user from novice- to expert-level interaction.

❑ Base design on the systemic view of the cognitive unit, artifact-human interaction.

Support creativity—adaptability, innovation, flexibility, and collaboration—as appropriate:

❑ Support adaptability—avoid functional fixedness by displaying how the i-f can be used for multiple purposes; design for maximum flexibility.

❑ Support innovation—design with requisite variety in mind to stimulate new thoughts and new combinations of thoughts.

❑ Support convenient collaboration.

In software design focus on the user's goals.

❑ Don't make the user look stupid.

❑ Don't rely on metaphors (use idioms) as they require too much interpretation.

❑ Don't design to the structure of the medium but to the user's goals.

❑ Don't stop the user from flowing through tasks.

❏   Focus on revenue- and goal-fulfilling tasks.

❏   Make the design of major screens subtle.

❏   Make the designs minor screens more elaborate.

In describing how to put these individual LCD principles to use, Table 10.2 charts the process of using them in an organized and systematic manner.

Table 10.2. Using the LCD Tools

LCD Process		Layering by Applying Principles of the Cognitive Hierarchy					
		Layer 1 Perception Principles	Layer 2 Mental Model	Layer 3 Categorization	Layer 4 Visualization	Layer 5 Expertise	Layer 6 Learning
Extending Design to Higher Levels of Complexity	Artifact Only	X	X	X	X	X	X
	Information-Field Individual-Object	Y	Y	Y	Y	Y	Y
	Information-Fields Collaborative Group-Objects	Z	Z	Z	Z	Z	Z

Using this tool kit guides the designer through a process of Extending and Layering, incrementally adding new cognitive layers of design prin-ciples over increasingly complex fields of human-artifact interaction. In the first pass, the designer runs through the layers of the design at the isolated object level marked with an x, then proceeds through the more interactive levels marked with a y, and ends, if appropriate, by going through the distributed interactive layers at the z level of object complexity.

NEW THINKING, NEW DESIGN, NEW WORLD

In an effort to focus some light on the management of complexity, I have explored the following: (a) the issue of cognitive complexity and its importance; (b) the nature of cognitive complexity, its sources, and characteristics; (c) the evaluation of information design in terms of managing complexity; (d) the relationship between areas of cognitive science and information science research; and (e) the concept of learner-centered design and its five perspectives (the cognitive hierarchy) on managing complexity while augmenting content and system competency. This exploration resides within a broader context of managing the complexity that has arisen in almost all avenues of life in this century and that shows no sign of abating in the next. It is the responsibility of the designer to reverse this trend and by designing for simplicity create a world more enjoyable and productive for all its inhabitants.

Context

In this century, we have had an assault on our view of the world as a simple place, but we have been given few means of thinking about it, let alone thriving on it. The last structured world of Newton has given way to relativity, quantum probabilities, Heisenberg's uncertainty, Gödel's incompleteness proof, fuzzy logic, analogue computing, and chaos theory. Our conceptualization of the world we live in has increasingly moved toward the gray and murky way the world really works and away from the stark simplistic contrast of the Aristotelian excluded middle. So what is to be done? How do we begin to learn to think about this "brave new complex world" where reality is actually getting more complex and science is beginning to confidently study it in all its dynamism and nonlinearity? First, we need to recognize that complexity is a concept itself and not just the characteristic of other things. Second, we need to understand that if complexity is working on the natural level it is also playing a role in the human design of human artifacts. This discussion of cognitive complexity has been meant to promote a recognition of the value of looking at complexity at the design level. It is only from insight at this level that we will come to manage complexity rather than letting it manage our learning and designing lives.

Conclusion

Any successful attempt to ameliorate the evolutionary complexification of our cognitive lives requires a two-pronged approach: (a) the application of cognitive strategies, individual and distributed, to arm individuals with adequate thinking skills in the face of complexity; and (b) the application of learner-centered principles that provide designers with a framework for managing cognitive complexity in information-field design. This book demonstrates that the cognitive and information sciences already have many of the tools to implement these learning strategies and design principles. Thus, we are ready to begin the transformation of our world experience into one that facilitates, rather than frustrates, our natural learning instincts to seek understanding.

Glossary of Key LCD Terms

The new circumstances under which we are placed call for new words, new phrases, and for the transfer of old words to new objects.

—Thomas Jefferson

Artifact

Anything that is made and designed by humans. In our context, this includes products for home or office, information designs such as maps and guides, electronic or computer-based information systems, or corporate workspaces/office designs. These are the designed objects of the person-object interaction I have termed an *interactive-information-field*.

Chaos Theory

In this context, a theory that explains the growth of complex entities from the interaction of very simple components and processes. It is a set of principles that explains and predicts a broad scope of phenomena that have been thought to be random or chaotic but that, in reality, are governed by laws. Chaos theory may be better termed *complexity science*, for it reveals order out of what seems to be chaos.

Cognitive Complexity

These are factors in our environment that make it difficult to understand how to use our artifacts effectively or efficiently. Complexity elements include societal forces such as rapid change and numerous social and informational interactions; information overload; difficult problems, such as poverty; complex systems, such as our environment; and incoherent design, design characterized by its useless complexity.

Complex

Difficult to understand. Intricate; so full of parts and the interrelationships between those parts that it is difficult to separate one from the other.

Constructivist

An approach to learning and instruction based on the work of Piaget and others. Its basic tenet in instruction is to consider students to be active co-constructors of their own understanding. This is opposed to the idea that students are empty vessels waiting to be filled up. Thus, under this scheme, learners are given a chance to discover understanding through inquiry rather than developing knowledge through the simple memorization of facts and figures.

Distributed Cognition

Refers to the idea that people do not operate as cognitive silos (separate cognitive units), totally independent from others, designed artifacts, and the culture that surrounds them. In LCD, this is the recognition that a user's interaction with an artifact forms a systemic (whole) unit. This unit carries the responsibility for the total cognitive capacity of making the person-object interaction understandable, effective, and engaging. In LCD, the person-object unit is called an interactive-information-field.

Environmentals

This object of design includes workspaces and corporate office layout along with furniture and other equipment, plus in a broader conception of design, such things as the Vietnam War Memorial, the Reagan Library, a corporate information center, or a museum like the Getty in Los Angeles.

I-F

See *Interactive-Information-Field.*

Information Design/Architect

After the work of Wurman and Tufte, this is the design process and presentation of information geared toward understanding and usefulness. This includes artifacts from the textual Smart Yellow Pages, to the graphic explanations of David Macaulay, and the design of whole environments.

Interactive-Information-Field

The frame of reference used in LCD; the communicative interaction between the designed object and the human. This frame of reference, borrowed from distributed cognition, focuses on distributing the neural load (the responsibility for understanding) between the user and the object being used. Information-fields are composed of human and designed artifacts. In this context, the "designed artifacts" are of three types: consumer and industrial products, information design and information systems, and workspaces and environments.

Heuristic

Reintroduced by Polya in his modern heuristic approach to solving math problems, a heuristic is a rule of thumb or a set of guidelines that supports problem solving and learning. It is any general guide to thinking that helps to direct one toward solutions without yielding a specific answer.

LCD

See *Learner-Centered Design.*

Learnability

In this context, *learnability* refers to the elements of design that help to get a user started using an artifact.

Learner-Centered Design (LCD)

This is an attitude or approach to design that views users of artifacts as active, participative learners seeking to understand the "what" and "how" of their environment. It is aimed at scaffolding or supporting users in gaining that understanding. It includes a set of design principles based on learnability, usability, and understandability, where *understandability* means not only a deep grasp of how to use something, the ability to interact with the design beyond a surface level, but also an understanding of the content or meaning conveyed by the system. LCD should be used on those objects of sufficient complexity as warranted. LCD extends understandability to the design of actual content (text, text flow, and graphics used within the artifact). It focuses on managing cognitive complexity and thus focuses on the design of artifacts that are of sufficient complexity to warrant the extra effort. The challenge of today is that a large percentage of our products do possess significant intricacy to be considered complex. It is important to note that LCD, in the context of this book, addresses the design of things other than computer-based learning systems (see *Interactive-information-field*).

Mental Model

A version of a knowledge structure, found in long-term memory, that holds the understanding of a topic or procedure. In learner- and user-centered design one of the key design and performance goals is to facilitate the development of a mental model of how an application works.

Metacognitive

This refers to the awareness one has of his or her own thinking processes. Metacognition comprises the monitoring or evaluative aspects of thinking. It is metacognition that selects a problem-solving method, monitors how successful it is, and changes to another method as appropriate. It is considered a key factor in learning success, along with domain knowledge, and higher-level thinking strategies. LCD should support metacognitive awareness.

Neural Load

In LCD, this refers to the amount of effort it takes to understand something. A basic tenet of LCD is that proper design makes the designed object responsible for carrying more and more of the neural load of the artifact-human interaction.

Scaffolding

Any of a wide variety of techniques to extend a learner to perform beyond his or her current knowledge and skill levels. These could include a just-in-time help system, mentoring, tutoring, training wheels on a bicycle, heuristics, or flying a plane with an instructor. In our LCD context, it broadly refers to any designed aids that support and facilitate the learning process.

Schema, Script, Frame

Like mental models these are versions of knowledge structures or how knowledge of different types are represented in long-term memory.

System-Content Competency

Understanding of the information provided within the system in terms of help screens, messages, displays, audio, video, hyperlinked text, and so on.

UCD

See *User-Centered Design*.

Understandability

This concept has two parts. First, it is an extension of usability principles to include understanding the product or system one is working with to such a level that the user can easily do all the things the design of the system might require. For example, a television set of the 1960s or 1970s requires no understandability of design. One can run it easily from the obvious surface cues, knobs, and so on. However, a television of the year 2000 will require understandability because its use in connecting with the Internet and a hundred other appliances will be too complicated to be left to regular design principles. Thus, understandability is especially applicable to the design of complex products from pagers to workspaces. Second, understandability is concerned with the adequacy of the actual content (text, graphics, examples, audio clips, and so on) in delivering understanding, in being instructional. This becomes very important as we increasingly add information into our products, systems, and spaces. It is the difference in importance between understanding how to navigate the nodes and links of the Internet and understanding the information that the Internet provides. The Internet's ultimate usefulness will reside with the quality and understandability of its content.

Usability

Design elements associated with ease of learning, efficiency of use, protection against errors, and comfort of use.

User-Centered Design

Developed in the 1980s by Donald Norman and others, this design philosophy was based on the tenet of moving design from being technology centered to being human centered. Its major tools are the application of cognitive-based design principles, with a special emphasis on facilitating mental models.

Workspace

The workplace is undergoing profound changes as we move to self-directed teams of independent knowledge workers. Collaborative problem solving is increasing. All this change is supported by a steady flow of information circulating through the workplace in terms of technology and increased human-to-human interaction. This whole new working environment is the "workspace." Those engaged in creating the workspaces of the future have a great opportunity to use integrated ergonomic and environmental designs to scaffold the cognitive capacities of teams that are often not ready to carry the increased load of decision making and information processing that is being demanded of them.

References

Adams, J. (1974). *Conceptual blockbusting*. Stanford, CA: Stanford Alumni Association.

Anderson, J. (1985). *Cognitive psychology*. New York: W. H. Freeman.

Andriole, S., & Adelman, L. (1995). *Cognitive systems engineering for user-computer interface design, prototyping, and evaluation*. Hillsdale, NJ: Lawrence Erlbaum.

Anzai, Y. (1991). Learning and use of representations for physics expertise. In K. Ericsson & J Smith (Eds.), *Toward a general theory of expertise* (pp. 64–92). Cambridge, UK: Cambridge University Press.

Baldonado, M., & Winograd, T. (1996). SenseMaker: An information-exploration interface supporting the contextual evolution of the user's interest. Stanford University Digital Library Initiative working paper. <http://www-diglib.stanford.edu/cgi-bin/wp/get/SIDL-WP-1996–0048>.

Banathy, B. H. (1991). *Systems design of education*. Englewood Cliffs, NJ: Educational Technologies Publications.

Barsalou, L. (1983). Ad hoc categories. *Memory and Cognition, 11*, 221–227.

Barsalou, L. (1992). *Cognitive psychology: An overview for cognitive scientists*. Hillsdale, NJ: Lawrence Erlbaum.

Bell, D. (1973). *The coming post industrial society*. New York: Basic Books.

Bigge, M. L. (1982). *Learning theories for teachers*. New York: HarperCollins.

Borgman, C. (1986). The user's mental model of an information retrieval system: An experiment on a prototype online catalog. *International Journal Man-Machine Studies, 34*, 47–64.

Bruer, J. T. (1993). *Schools for thought*. Cambridge: MIT Press.

Buckland, M. (1991). *Information and information systems*. New York: Praeger.

Card, S., Moran, J., & Newell, A. (1983). *The psychology of human-computer interaction.* Hillsdale, NJ: Lawrence Erlbaum.

Card, S. & Moran, T. (1995). User technology: From pointing to pondering. In R. Baecker, J. Grudin, W. Buxton, & S. Greenberg (Eds.), *Readings in human-computer interaction: Toward the year 2000* (2nd). San Francisco: Morgan Kaufmann.

Ceci, S., & Ruiz, A. (1992). The role of general ability in cognitive complexity: A case study of expertise. In R. Hoffman (Ed.); *The psychology of expertise: Cognitive research and empirical AI* (pp. 218–230). New York: Springer-Verlag.

Checkland, P. (1981). *Systems thinking, systems practice.* New York: John Wiley.

Chen, H., & Dhar, V. (1991). Cognitive process as a basis for intelligent retrieval systems design. *Information Processing and Management, 27,* 405–422.

Cohen, J., & Stewart, I. (1994). *The collapse of chaos.* New York: Viking.

Collins, C., & Mangieri, J. (Eds.). (1992). *Teaching thinking.* Hillsdale, NJ: Lawrence Erlbaum.

Cooper, A. (1995). *About face.* Foster City: Programmer's Press.

Cooper, A. (1999). *The inmates are running the asylum.* Indianapolis: Sams Publishing.

Cousins, S. (1996). A task oriented interface to a digital library. Stanford University Digital Library Initiative working paper. <http://www-diglib.stanford.edu/diglib/WP/PUBLIC/DOC44.html>.

Cowan, N. (1995). *Attention and memory: An integrated framework.* Oxford, UK: Oxford University Press.

Crane, H., & Rtischev, D. (1993). Pen and voice unite. *Byte, 10,* 98–102.

Cremmins, E. (1982). *The art of abstracting.* Philadelphia: ISI.

Csikszentmihalyi, M. (1993). *The evolving self.* New York: HarperCollins.

D'Andrade, R. (1995). *The development of cognitive anthropology.* Cambridge, UK: Cambridge University Press.

Daniels, P. (1986). Cognitive models in information retrieval: An evaluative review. *Journal of Documentation, 42,* 272–304.

de Bono, E. (1970). *Lateral thinking.* New York: Harper & Row.

Dillon, A. (1996). Myths, misconceptions, and an alternative perspective on information usage and the electronic medium. In J. Rouet, J. Levonen, A. Dillon, & R. Spiro (Eds.), *Hypertext and cognition,* (pp. 25–42). Mahwah, NJ: Lawrence Erlbaum.

Dörner, D. (1983). Heuristics and cognition in complex systems. In R. Groner, M. Groner, & W. Bischof (Eds.), *Methods of heuristics* (pp. 89–107). Hillsdale, NJ: Lawrence Erlbaum.

Ehrlich, K. (1996). Applied mental models in human-computer interaction. In J. Oakhill & A. Garnham (Eds.), *Mental models in cognitive science* (pp. 223–246). Hove, UK: Psychology Press.

Esperet, E. (1996). Notes on hypertext, cognition, and language. In J. Rouet, J. Levonen, A. Dillon, & R. Spiro (Eds.), *Hypertext and cognition*, (pp. 149–156). Mahwah, NJ: Lawrence Erlbaum.

Estes, W. (1994). *Classification and cognition*. Oxford, UK: Oxford University Press.

Farooq, M. & Dominick, W. (1988). A survey of formal tools and models for developing user interfaces. *International Journal Man-Machine Studies, 29*, 479–496.

Flood, R., & Carson, E. (1990). *Dealing with complexity*. New York: Plenum.

Foley, M., & Hart, A. (1991). Expert-novice differences and knowledge elicitation. In R. Hoffman (Ed.), *The psychology of expertise: Cognitive research and empirical AI* (pp. 233–244). New York: Springer-Verlag.

Foltz, P. (1996). Comprehension, coherence, and strategies in hypertext and linear text. In J. Rouet, J. Levonen, A. Dillon, and R. Spiro (Eds.), *Hypertext and cognition* (pp. 109–136). Mahwah, NJ: Lawrence Erlbaum.

Friedman, M., & Carterette, E. (Eds.). (1996). *Cognitive ecology*. San Diego: Academic Press.

Funke, J. (1991). Solving complex problems: Exploration and control of complex social problems. In R. Sternberg & P. Frensch (Eds.), *Complex problem solving* (pp. 185–222). Hillsdale, NJ: Lawrence Erlbaum.

Furnas, G. W. (1986). Generalized fisheye views. In *Human Factors in Computing Systems CHI '86 conference proceedings*, Boston, ACM, 16–23.

Furnas, G. W. (1991). New graphical reasoning models for understanding graphical interfaces. In *Human Factors in Computing Systems chi '91 conference proceedings*, New Orleans, ACM, 71–78.

Furnas, G. W., & Bederson, B. (1995). Space-scale diagrams: Understanding multiscale interfaces. In *Human Factors in Computing Systems CHI '95 conference proceedings*, Denver, ACM, 234–241.

Furnas, G. W., & Zacks, J. (1994). Multitrees: Enriching and reusing hierarchical structure. In *Human Factors in Computing Systems CHI '94 conference proceedings*, Boston, ACM, 330–336.

Gardner, H. (1985). *The mind's new science: A history of the cognitive revolution.* New York: Basic Books.

Gergen, K. (1991). *The saturated self.* New York: Basic Books.

Goerner, S. (1990). Chaos and the evolving ecology world hypothesis: Implications for just systems. in *Proceedings of the 34th International Society of Systems Science*, Portland, ISSS, 433–446.

Gove, P. (Ed.). (1986). *Webster's third international dictionary.* Springfield, MA: Merriam-Webster.

Guillemette, R. (1989). Development and validation of a reader-based documentation measure. *International Journal Man-Machine Studies, 30*, 551–574.

Halfhill, T. (1997). Good-bye, GUI, hello, NUI. *Byte, 22*, (7), 60–72.

Halpern, D. (1996). *Thinking critically about critical thinking.* Mahwah, NJ: Lawrence Erlbaum.

Holland, J., Holyoak, K., Nisbett, R., & Thagard, P. (1986). *Induction: Processes of inference, learning, and discovery.* Cambridge: MIT Press.

Hurd, M. (1991). *Dialectical reasoning in the adult years.* Unpublished doctoral dissertation, Saybrook Institute, San Francisco.

Hutchins, E. (1995). *Cognition in the wild.* Cambridge; MIT Press.

Hymes, C. (1997). *Classification in Object-Oriented Programming.* Unpublished dissertation proposal, University of Michigan, Ann Arbor.

Jacob, E. (1991). Classification and categorization: Drawing the line. In *Proceedings of the 2nd ASIS SIG/CR Classification Research Workshop,* 67–81.

Jefferies, R., Miller, J., Wharton, C., & Uyeda, K. (1991). User interface evaluation in the real world: A comparison of four techniques. In *Human Factors in Computing Systems CHI '91 conference proceedings,* New Orleans, ACM, 119–124.

Johnson-Laird, P. (1990). Mental models. In M. Posner (Ed.), *Foundations of cognitive science,* (pp. 469–500). Cambridge: MIT Press.

Kepner, C., & Tregoe, B. (1981). *The new rational manager.* Princeton, NJ: Princeton Research Press.

Kieras, D., & Bovair, S. (1984
ate a device. *Cognitive Science, 8,* 255–273.

Kieras, D., & Polson, P. (1985). An approach to the formal analysis of user complexity. *International Journal of Man-Machine Studies, 22,* 365–394.

Kirkpatrick, A. (1997). Personal communication.

Klapp, O. (1986). *Overload and boredom.* Westport, CT: Greenwood.

Kosslyn, S. (1996). *Image and brain.* Cambridge: MIT Press.

Kuhlthau, C. (1991). Inside the search process: Information seeking from the user's perspective. *Journal of the American Society of Information Science, 42,* 361–371.

Lakoff, G., & Johnson, M. (1980). *Metaphors to live by.* Chicago: University of Chicago Press.

Landsdale, M., & Ormerod, T. (1994). *Understanding interfaces: A handbook of human-computer dialogue.* London: Academic Press.

Laszlo, E. (1987). *Evolution: The grand synthesis.* Boston: Shambhala.

Legrenzi, P., & Girotto, V. (1996). Mental models in reasoning and decision making processes. In J. Oakhill & A. Garnham (Eds.), *Mental models in cognitive science* (pp. 95–118). Hove, UK: Psychology Press.

Lesgold, A., & Lajoie, S. (1991). Complex problem solving in electronics. In R. Sternberg & P. Frensch (Eds.), *Complex problem solving* (pp. 287–316). Hillsdale, NJ: Lawrence Erlbaum.

Madsen, K. (1994). A guide to metaphorical design. *Communications of the ACM, 37* (12) 57–61.

Marchionini, G. (1995). *Information seeking in electronic environments*. Cambridge, UK: Cambridge University Press.

Marcus, A. (1993). Human communications issues in advanced UI. *Communications of the ACM, 36* (4) 101–108.

Marshall, S. (1995). *Schemas in problem solving*. Cambridge, UK: Cambridge University Press.

Mayer, R. (1983). *Thinking, problem solving, cognition*. New York: W. H. Freeman.

Moran, T. (1981). An applied psychology of the user. ACM *Computing Surveys, 13*, 1–11.

Mullet, K., & Sano, D. (1995). *Designing visual interfaces*. Mountain View, CA: SunSoft.

Newell, A. & Card, S. (1985). The prospects for psychological science in human-computer interaction. *Human-Computer Interaction, 1*, 209–242.

Newell, A., & Simon, H. A. (1972). *Human problem solving*. Englewood Cliffs, NJ: Prentice Hall.

Nicolis, G., & Prigogine, I. (1989). *Exploring complexity*. New York: W. H. Freeman.

Nielsen, J. (1992). Finding usability problems through heuristic evaluation. In *Human Factors in Computing Systems CHI '92 conference proceedings*, Monterey, ACM, 373–392.

Nielsen, J. (1993). *Hypertext and hypermedia*. Boston: Academic Press.

Nielsen, J. (1995). *Multimedia and hypertext*. Boston: Academic Press.

Nielsen, J., & Molich, R. (1990). Heuristic evaluation of user interfaces. In *Human Factors in Computing Systems CHI '90 conference proceedings*, Seattle, ACM, 249–256.

Norman, D. (1986). Cognitive engineering. In D. Norman & S. Draper (Eds.), *User centered system design* (pp. 31–61). Hillsdale, NJ: Lawrence Erlbaum.

Norman, D. (1988). *The psychology of everyday things*. New York: Basic Books.

Norman, D. (1993). *Things that make us smart*. New York: Addison-Wesley.

Norman, D., & Draper, S. (Eds.). (1986). *User centered system design*. Hillsdale, N J: Lawrence Erlbaum.

Norman, D., & Spohrer, J. (1996). Learner-centered education. *Communications of the ACM, 39* (4), 24–27.

Olson, J., & Biolsi, K. (1991). Techniques for representing expert knowledge. In K. Ericsson & J. Smith (Eds.), *Toward a general theory of expertise* (pp. 240–285). Cambridge, UK: Cambridge University Press.

Olson, J., & Nilsen, E. (1987). Analysis of the cognition involved in spreadsheet software interaction. *Human-Computer Interaction, 3*, 309–349.

Paepcke, A. (1996, May). Digital libraries: Searching is not enough. What we learned on site. *D-LIB magazine*, Stanford University. <http://www.dlib.org/dlib/may96/stanford/05paepcke/html.>

Patel, V., & Groen, G. (1991). The general and specific nature of medical expertise: A critical look. In K. Ericsson & J. Smith (Eds.), *Toward a general theory of expertise* (pp. 93–125). Cambridge, UK: Cambridge University Press.

Paul, R. (1990). *Critical thinking.* Rohnert Park, CA: Center for Critical Thinking and Moral Critique.

Pea, R. (1993). Distributed intelligence and designs for education. In G. Salomon (Ed.), *Distributed cognitions: Psychological and educational considerations* (pp. 47–87). Cambridge, UK: Cambridge University Press.

Peat, D. (1985). *Artificial intelligence: How machines think.* New York: Baen Enterprises.

Perry, W. (1970). *Forms of intellectual and ethical development in the college years.* New York: Holt, Rinehart & Winston.

Piaget, J. (1954). *The construction of reality in the child.* New York: Basic Books.

Polson, P. (1988). The consequences of consistent and inconsistent user interfaces. In R. Guindon (Ed.), *Cognitive science and its applications for human-computer interaction* (pp. 59–108). Hillsdale, NJ: Lawrence Erlbaum.

Polya, G. (1985). *How to solve it.* Princeton, NJ: Princeton University Press.

Posner, M. (1990). *Foundations of cognitive science.* Cambridge: MIT Press.

Prigogine, I., & Stengers, I. (1984). *Order out of chaos.* New York: Bantam.

Reeves, W. (1996). *Cognition and complexity.* Lanham, MD: Scarecrow .

Rosch, E. (1978). Principles of categorization. In E. Rosch & B. Lloyd (Eds.), *Cognition and categorization* (pp. 27–48). Hillsdale, NJ: Lawrence Erlbaum.

Rouet, J., Levonen, J., Dillon, A. and Spiro, R. (Eds.). (1996). *Hypertext and cognition.* Mahwah, NJ: Lawrence Erlbaum.

Rubinstein, M. (1986). *Tools for thinking and problem solving.* Englewood Cliffs, NJ: Prentice Hall.

Rudnicky, A. (1993). Matching the input mode to the task. *Byte, 10,* 100.

Salomon, G. (Ed.). (1993). *Distributed cognitions: Psychological and educational considerations.* Cambridge, UK: Cambridge University Press.

Scardamalia, M. & Bereiter, C. (1991). Literate expertise. In K. Ericsson & J. Smith (Eds.), *Toward a general theory of expertise* (pp. 172–194). Cambridge, UK: Cambridge University Press.

Schank, R. (1997). *Virtual learning.* New York: McGraw-Hill.

Schumacher, R., & Czerwinski, M. (1991). Mental models and the acquisition of expert knowledge. In R. Hoffman (Ed.), *The psychology of expertise: Cognitive research and empirical AI* (pp. 61–79). New York: Springer-Verlag.

Senge, P. M. (1990). *The fifth discipline.* Garden City, NY: Doubleday.

Shenk, D. (1997). *Data smog.* San Francisco: HarperEdge.

Shneiderman, B. (1992). *Designing the user interface: Strategies for effective human-computer interaction.* Reading, MA: Addison-Wesley.

Sokal, R. (1974). Classification: purposes, principles, progress, prospects. *Science, 185,* 115–123.

Soloway, E., Guzdial, M., & Hay, K. (1994, April). Learner-centered design. *Interactions, 1* (2), 37-48.

Soloway, E. & Pryor, A. (1996). The next generation in human-computer interaction. *Communications of the ACM, 39* (4), 16–17.

Solso, R. (1994). *Cognition and the visual arts.* Cambridge: MIT Press.

Stein, J. (Ed.). (1982) *Random House college dictionary.* New York: Random House.

Sternberg, R. (1990a). *Metaphors of mind.* Cambridge, UK: Cambridge University Press.

Sternberg, R. (Ed.). (1990b). *Wisdom: its nature, origins and development.* Cambridge, UK: Cambridge University Press.

Strunk, W., Jr., & White, E. B. (1979). *The elements of style.* (3rd ed.). New York: Macmillan.

Tanin, E., Beigel, R., & Shneiderman, B. (1996). Incremental data structures and algorithms for dynamic query interfaces. *SIGMOD Record, 25* (4), 21–24.

Toffler, A. (1970). *Future shock.* New York: Bantam Books.

Treu, S. (1994). *User interface evaluation.* New York: Plenum.

Trikha, M. (1997, January 14). Browsers hailed as new wave. *San Jose Mercury News,* p. I–C.

Tufte, E. (1990). *Envisioning information.* Cheshire, CT: Graphics Press.

Tufte, E. (1997). *Visual explanations.* Cheshire, CT: Graphics Press.

von Bertalanffy, L. (1968). *General systems theory.* New York: George Braziller.

Voss, J., Wolfe, C., Lawrence, J., & Engle, R. (1991). From representation to decision: An analysis of problem solving in international relations. In R. Sternberg & P. Frensch (Eds.), *Complex problem solving* (pp. 119–158). Hillsdale, NJ: Lawrence Erlbaum.

Wurman, R. S. (1989). *Information anxiety.* New York: Random House.

Wurman, R. S. (1997). *Information architects.* New York: Graphis.

Yates, F. (1978). Complexity and the limits to knowledge. *American Journal of Physiology, 4,* R201–R204.

Index

About the Author

Wayne W. Reeves has served as the project manager and content architect for a variety of intranets at Sun Microsystems including SunWeb, Sun's first corporate intranet. He was also the founding Manager of the eLibrary and Information Services for Sun and the Manager of Engineering Information Development, Engineering Training, and Library Services for Siemens, IBM, and ROLM. He holds a bachelor of arts degree in philosophy from the University of California, Santa Cruz, a master's in psychology from Lone Mountain College, and a doctorate in human science/cognitive systems from the Saybrook Graduate Institute. He is currently an adjunct professor at San Jose State University's School of Library and Information Science, a creative thinking advocate, and a consulting cognitive architect, focusing on information design in corporate training, design, and knowledge management solutions.